IRead For Life

Welcome to your
Pre-Reader Phonics

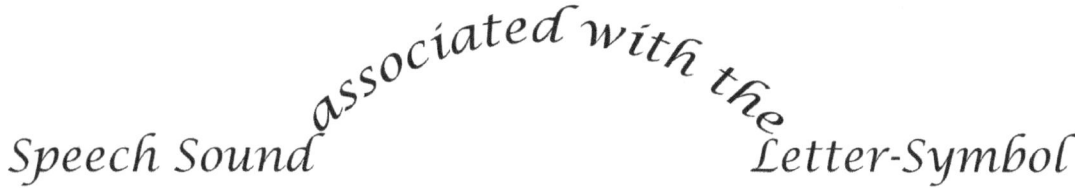
Speech Sound associated with the Letter-Symbol

Vinnette Mae Glidden, M.S.
Speech & Language Pathologist

Illustrated by Vinnette Mae Glidden
Edited by Charles Glidden

Scribes Ltd

Copyright © 2021 Vinnette Mae Glidden   Pre-Reader Phonics

Copyright © 2013, 2021 Vinnette Mae Glidden
Previous copyright © 1995, 2011
Illustrations Copyright © 2013, 2021 Vinnette Mae Glidden except:
Xylophone: Courtesy WPClipart, wpclipart.com

All Rights Reserved.
No part of this book may be copied, reproduced or transmitted in any form or by any means, electronic or mechanical including photocopying, scanning, recording or by any information storage and retrieval system or otherwise, without written permission of the publisher except in the case of brief quotations embodied in critical reviews and certain other noncommercial uses permitted by copyright law.

Published 2021 by *Scribes Ltd.*
24 Huldah Ave.
Suite D
George Town, Grand Cayman, Cayman Islands

Inquiries should be sent to:
Email: admin@ireadforlife.ky
Telephone: 1-345-947-1497

Scribes Ltd.
PO Box 1993
Grand Cayman KY1-1104
CAYMAN ISLANDS

Website: www.ireadforlife.ky

ISBN 978-1-9196499-0-0

Printed in the United States of America

Your Guide

Thank you for choosing the IRead For Life series of workbooks. The effectiveness of this workbook and the IRFL approach is dependent on the facilitator knowing how to say the speech sounds in isolation correctly. Whether you are a parent or a qualified teacher, we strongly recommend that you purchase the video series *Sounds and Symbols – A fun way to learn to read!* which is available on DVD from Amazon® and the IRead For Life Center. You can also stream *Sounds and Symbols* from the *ireadforlife.ky* and *Vimeo.com* websites. A tutorial of the speech sounds associated with the letter-symbols begins each video. These videos will serve as an entertaining supplement for the children as they learn to read.

First Day
Start with clapping hands and singing a song relating to hands. Color the hands. Talk about hands as a body part with ten fingers. Introduce the Land of Make Believe. Have the children draw a picture of themselves or paste a photo of themselves in the picture frame.

Second Day
Introduce the Vowel family and have the children trace the vowel symbols and color the family house. Talk about what constitutes a house – the floor, walls, roof, ceiling, windows, etc. Compare a house for people in real life and/or in the Land of Make Believe with the homes of other creatures.

Every Day
Begin each day with a happy song that involves the children clapping their hands.
- Have the children write their name and the date.
- Trace the letter-symbols in the picture frame.
- Color the picture frame.
- Write the letter-symbols on the lines provided.
- Read the directions on the next page with the children and have them do the task.
- Then, emphasize the sound that you are introducing by having the students color the related pictures and complete the tasks on the pages that follow. The students should say the speech sound or the word whenever they do a matching exercise. Remember to read the instructions with the children.
- A fun task that you may like to give the children is to create a mosaic color pattern in the picture frame.

Remember! – Facilitators must begin to expose students to letter-symbols as early as possible. They must ensure that students grasp the concept that letter-symbols represent speech sounds and that letter-symbols form written words. It is very important that students understand that the words we write represent the words we speak.

Here are some ideas that facilitators can use to help children learn the association between speech sounds and letter-symbols:
- give each child finger-paint to write the letter-symbols of the speech sound the facilitator says
- use popsicle sticks, play dough or clay to make the letter-symbol being taught

To develop auditory training, a word box is provided for the facilitator to dictate age appropriate words for the student to write in the box.

About the IRFL approach to teaching reading

The IRead For Life method of "speech sound associated with the letter-symbol" is the basis for the series of seven workbooks in the IRFL program, beginning with the *Pre-Reader Phonics* workbook. The program is consistent in its presentation throughout the series. The IRead For Life program is used at the IRead For Life Center. For more than a decade, it has successfully made struggling readers good readers and good readers excellent readers.

The philosophy of the IRFL method is based on the fact that a child hears all of the speech sounds from the first day of life. Therefore, all the letter-symbols associated with the 44 speech sounds should be presented to children as a whole from day one of learning to read. The essence of the IRFL approach is "repetition, repetition, repetition" of the speech sound associated with the letter-symbol. Repeated enough times, "the speech sound associated with the letter-symbol" becomes indelibly imprinted on the open minds of young children. Using flashcards, all the speech sound/letter-symbol associations are presented in an easy, friendly fashion right out of the gate.

The exercises in this workbook provide practice in the following areas:
- understanding letter-symbols in groups to help organize the mind to make the association with speech sounds when seen in words
- decoding of words
- writing
- early understanding of what is a word and what is a sentence

The exercises are dependent on teacher/facilitator involvement. The lessons are directly associated with building auditory conceptualization, which is an essential requirement for good reading and spelling.

Teacher's Notes

Contents

Vowel Family House 1

Short Vowel Letter-symbols

a-................. 2 – 6   e-............... 31 – 34

i-................ 66 – 68   o-............. 109 – 112

u-............. 162 – 165   y-............. 176 – 179

Long Vowel / diphthongs/digraph Letter-symbols

ai ay a-e eigh................. 7 – 10   ea ey ee ei e-e eo -y ...... 35 – 40

I ie igh i-e -y .... 69 – 74   Oa oe o-e -o -ow .... 113 – 118

ue u-e ew eu –u .... 166 – 169   au aw augh .... 17 – 19

ou ow ough .... 122 – 126   oo ui -u (as in hoot gnu suit) .... 127 – 130

oo u (as in look & full) .... 131 – 133   oi oy .... 134 – 136

Modified Vowel Letter-symbols

ar (as in car) .... 11 – 13   are air aer- .... 14 – 16

eer ere .... 41 – 44   er ir ur ear .... 45 – 50

-ar --or -er -ure .... 51 – 54   or (as in horse) .... 119 – 121

Consonant Letter-symbols

B b	20 – 22	ch -tch -ture	23 – 26
D d	27 – 30	F f ph	55 – 58
G g –gh –gue	59 – 62	H h	63 – 65
J j -dge ge gi gy	75 – 80	K -ck C k -que	81 – 86
Qu qu	87 – 90	-X	91 – 93
L l	94 – 96	M m -mn -mb	97 – 101
N n kn- gn	102 – 105	-ng -nk –nc –nx –ng-	106 – 108
P p	137 – 140	R r rh wr	141 – 145
S -se ps- ci ce cy	146 – 150	Sh ti ci ssi	151 – 155
T t pt	156 – 158	Th th	159 – 161
V -ve	170 – 172	W wh	173 – 175
Y y	176 – 179	Z X--	180 – 182
-sia –sion –sure	183 – 185		

Exercises

Recognizing Words 186

Patterns –What is next? .... 187 – 189

Introduction to the Land of Make Believe Jailhouse ..... 190 – 191

Feet 192

My Book Log 193

Notes 194

Good Job 196

I can clap.

Land of Make Believe

Name: _____

Date: _____

This is my picture.

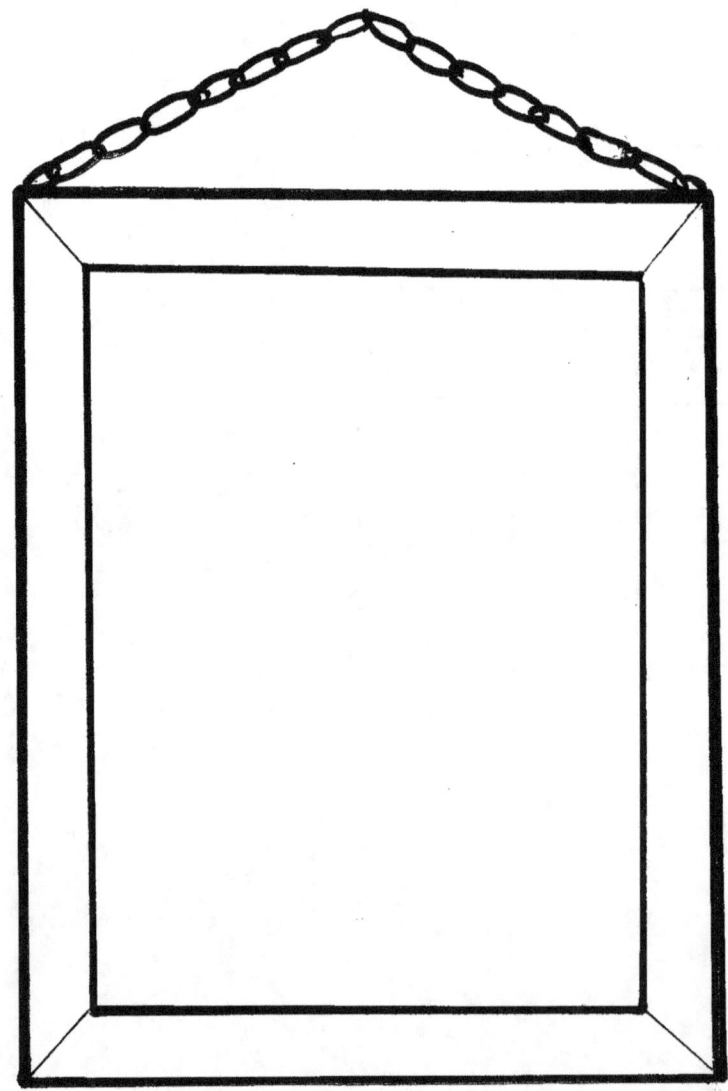

Name: _____

Date: _____

My first words

I	will
a / A	This
the	see
you	boy
can	girl
am	in

The facilitator should use these words in sentence strips to build sentences on a daily basis.

Example:

I can see a <u>fish</u>____.

I can see the <u>boy</u>____.

You can see a <u>cup</u>____.

You can see the <u>girl</u>____.

Copyright © 2021 Vinnette Mae Glidden   Pre-Reader Phonics

Name: _____

Date: _____

In the Land of Make Believe

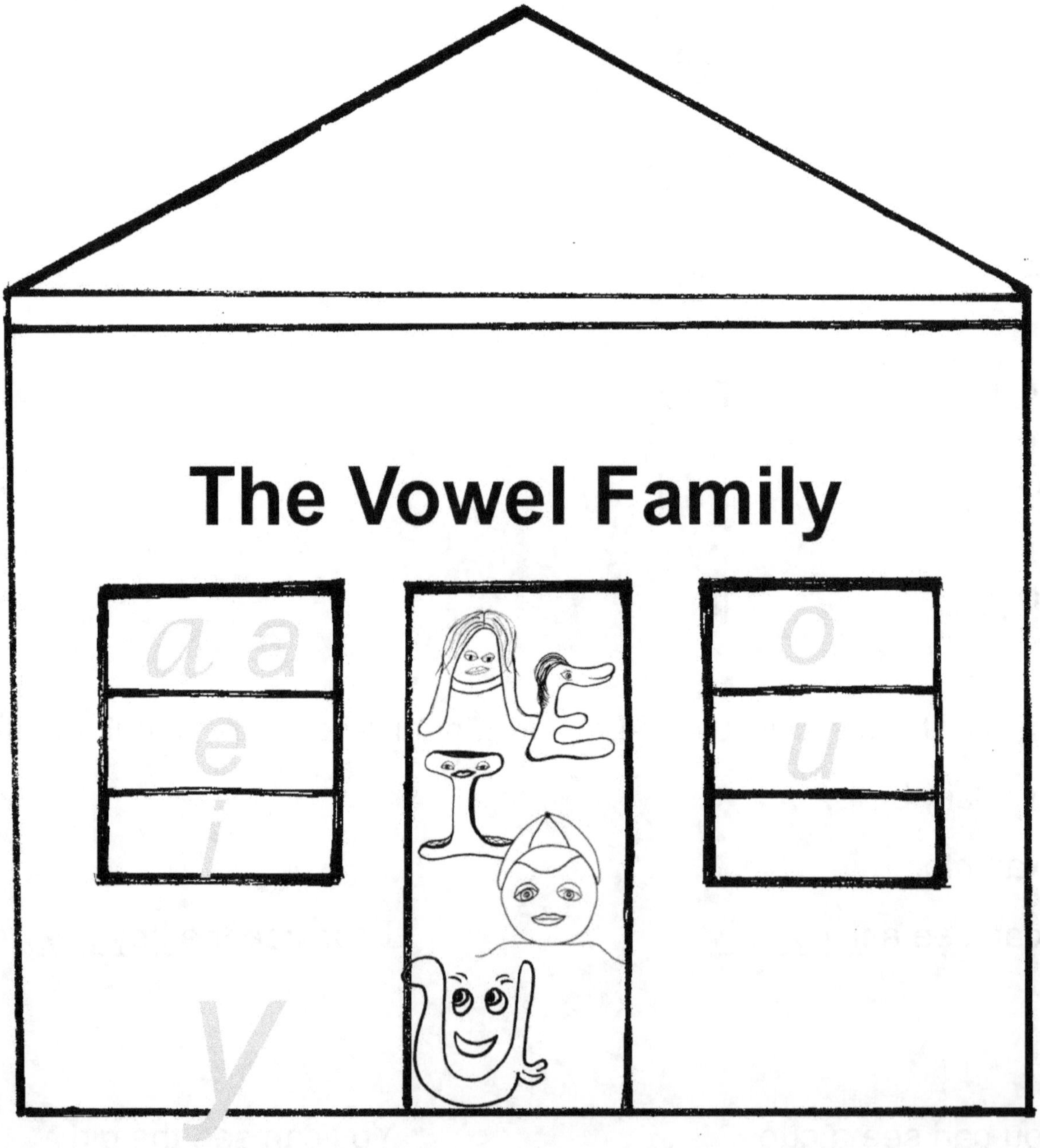

The Vowel Family

Copyright © 2021 Vinnette Mae Glidden   Pre-Reader Phonics

Name: _____

Date: _____

Tell the story "Anna the Opera Singer".

Color the picture of Anna.

I am Anna.

I can sing.

Name: _____

Date: _____

Color the picture frame.
Trace the letter-symbol.
Say the sound.
Write the letter-symbols.

uppercase _____

lowercase _____

lowercase _____

Letter-symbol

A a
a

Copyright © 2021 Vinnette Mae Glidden Pre-Reader Phonics Page 3

Name: _____

Date: _____

Draw a circle around the letter-symbols and the pictures. Draw a line to match the picture and letter-symbols that are alike. Say the sound for the letter-symbol as you draw the line.

a

a

A

a

a

A

a

Write the uppercase letter-symbol. _____

Write the lowercase letter-symbol. _____

Name: _____

Date: _____

Color the picture of the c**a**t.

Find the letter-symbols **a A** in each word and color them yellow. Say the words.

am   can   cat   Anna

Name: _____

Date: _____

Color the picture of the rat.

Draw lines to match the words that are the same:

cat   rat

rat   at

at   cat

Name:

Date:

Color the picture frame.
Trace the letter-symbols.
Say the sound.
Write the letter-symbols.

Letter-symbol

ai   ay
a-e
eigh
aigh

Tell the story called "A - Vowel and Friends".

Name: _____

Date: _____

Draw a circle around the letter-symbols and the pictures. Draw a line to match the picture and letter-symbols that are alike. Say the sound for the letter-symbol as you draw the line.

Can you tell the <u>A-Vowel and Friends</u> story? Say the A-Vowel cheer with your teacher.

e - i - g - h who do you appreciate?
a - i ... a - y look how we can educate.
a - e ... a - i - g - h now we can associate.
e - i - g - h   /ay ☀ ☀ /   a - i ... a - y /ay ☀ ☀ /
a - i - g - h /ay ☀ ☀ /
a - e /ay ☀ ☀ / Horaaaay!

Name: _____

Date: _____

Draw a circle around the letter-symbols and the pictures. Draw a line to match the picture and letter-symbols that are alike. Say the sound for the letter-symbol as you draw the line.

   a-e

eigh   eigh

a-e

Find the letter-symbols **eigh, a-e** in the words and color them yellow. Say the words.

eight   cake   take   make

Name: _____

Date: _____

Color the number **eigh**t.

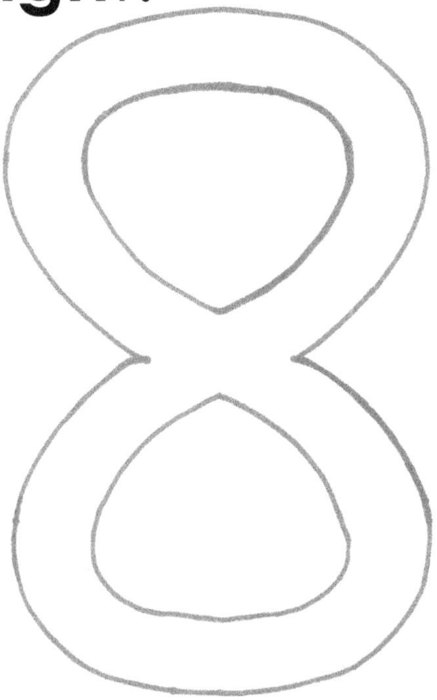

Draw a line to match the words that are the same.

day   tail

say   rain

rain   day

tail   say

Name: _____

Date: _____

Color the picture frame.
Trace the letter-symbols.
Say the sound.
Write the letter-symbols.

Letter-symbol

ar

ar

Can you tell the story "Arrrr! Says the Pirate"?

Name: _____

Date: _____

Draw a circle around the pictures and letter-symbols. Draw a line to match the pictures and letter-symbols. Say the sound for the letter-symbol as you draw the line.

ar

ar

Find the letter-symbols **ar** in each word and color them yellow. Say the words.

Mark   far   jar   art

Name: _____

Date: _____

Color the c**ar**.

This is a car.
Mark has a car.

Name: _____

Date: _____

Color the picture frame.
Trace the letter-symbols.
Say the sound.
Write the letter-symbols.

Letter-symbol

are

air

aer-

Can you tell the "A-Vowel Relaxes" story?

Name: _____

Date: _____

Draw a circle around the letter-symbols and pictures. Draw a line to match the pictures and letter-symbols that are alike. Say the sound for the letter-symbol as you draw the line.

air

are

aer-

are

air

aer-

Name: _____

Date: _____

Color the picture of the **air**plane.

Draw a line to match the words that are the same.

eight	air
air	car
car	eight

Name: _____

Date: _____

Color the picture frame.
Trace the letter-symbols.
Say the sound.
Write the letter-symbols.

Letter-symbol

au
aw
augh

U-Vowel exclaimed, "Aw! My goodness, where can that puppy be?"
Can you tell the story that this is from?

Name: _____

Date: _____

Draw a circle around the letter-symbols and pictures. Draw a line to match the pictures and letter-symbols that are alike. Say the sound for the letter-symbol as you draw the line.

au

aw   augh

[picture]   au

augh   aw

Name: _____

Date: _____

Color the **au**tumn leaves.

Draw a line to match the words that are the same.

Autumn	draw
draw	saw
saw	Autumn

Name: _____

Date: _____

Color the picture frame.
Trace the letter-symbols.
Say the sound.
Write the letter-symbols.

Letter-symbol

uppercase
_____
_____

lowercase
_____
_____

B b

Tell the story called "The Little Fish Bubbles".

Name: _____

Date: _____

Draw a circle around the letter-symbols and pictures. Draw a line to match the pictures and letter-symbols that are alike. Say the sound for the letter-symbol as you draw the line.

B

b

B

b

Find the letter-symbols **b B** in the words and color them yellow.

bat   bay   cab   Bob

Name: _____

Date: _____

Color the picture.

Write the letter-symbol **b** on the small bubbles. Then write a capital **B** on the big bubbles.

Name: _____

Date: _____

Color the picture frame.
Trace the letter-symbols.
Say the sound.
Write the letter-symbols.

Letter-symbol

ch
-tch
-ture

Can you tell the story "The Two Brothers C and H"?

Name: _____

Date: _____

Draw a circle around the pictures and letter-symbols. Draw a line to match the pictures and letter-symbols. Say the sound for the letter-symbols as you draw the line.

-ture

-tch

ch

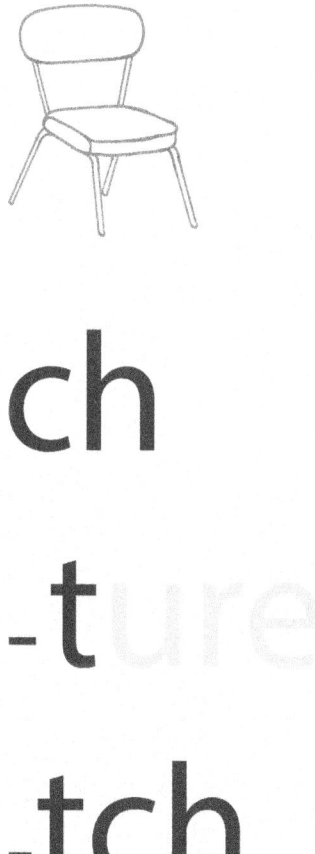

ch

-ture

-tch

Name: _____

Date: _____

Color the sat**ch**el.

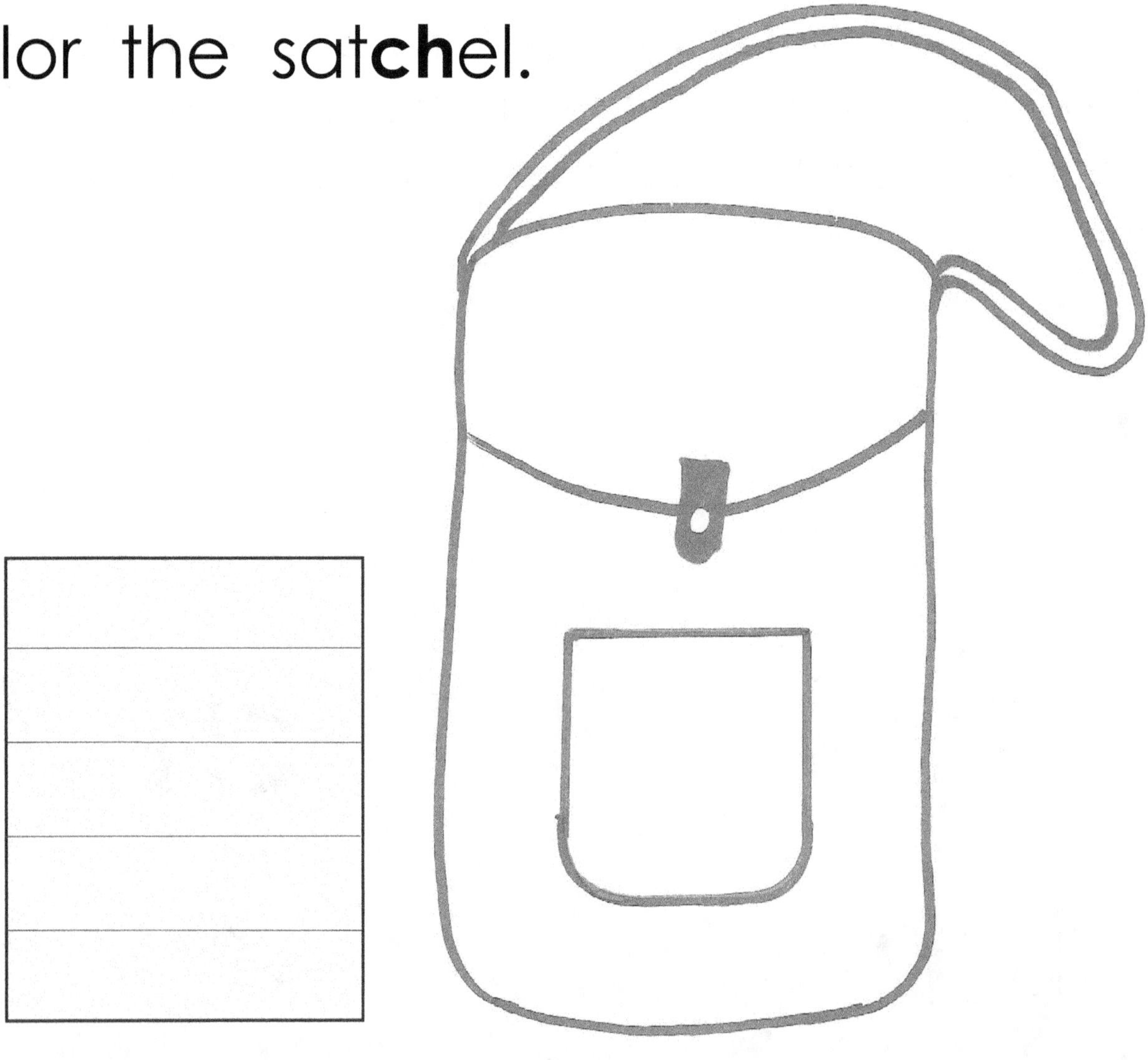

Find the letter-symbols **tch ch** in the words and color them yellow.

match   satchel   chat   chair

Name: _____

Date: _____

Color the picture.

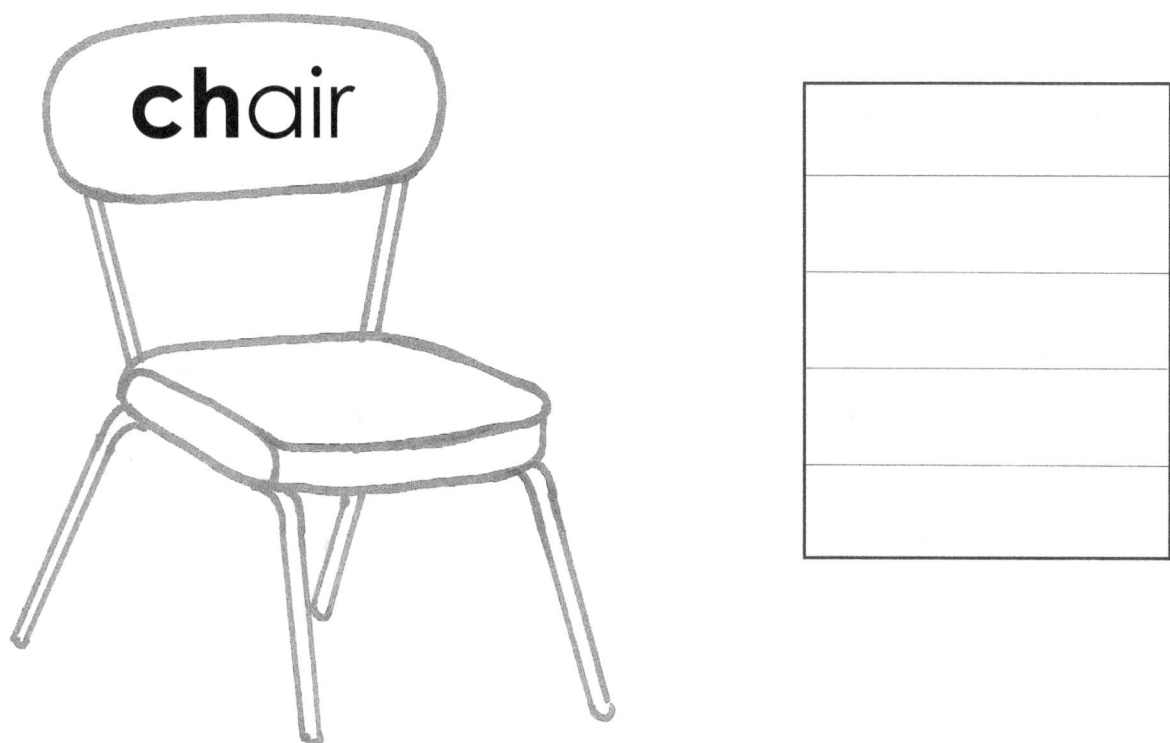

Say the word. Then draw a line to the word that is the same.

chair			match

picture			chair

match			picture

Name: _____

Date: _____

Color the picture frame.
Trace the letter-symbols.
Say the sound.
Write the letter-symbols.

uppercase
_____

lowercase
_____

Letter-symbol

D d

Can you tell the story "Big Daddy Consonant"?

Name: _____

Date: _____

Draw a circle around the pictures and letter-symbols. Draw a line to match the pictures and letter-symbols. Say the sound for the letter-symbols as you draw the line.

D   D

d

d

Write uppercase D _____

Write lowercase d _____

Name: _____

Date: _____

Color the picture of the **d**og.

Find the letter-symbols **d D** in the words and color them yellow.

add   Dad   bad   Dan

Name: _____

Date: _____

Color the pictures.

Write the name for the pictures.

This is Dora.

Dora is Anna's doll.

Dora
_____
_____

I see a duck in the pond.

duck
_____
_____

Name: _____

Date: _____

Etty begins with uppercase **E**.

Color the picture of **E**tty.

I am Etty.

I can read.

I can make the sound eh...eh.

Name: _____

Date: _____

Color the picture frame.
Trace the letter-symbols.
Say the sound.
Write the letter-symbols.

lowercase
_____

uppercase
_____

lowercase
_____

Letter-symbol

E-
e-
e-

Tell the story titled "Etty Meets E-Vowel".

Name: _____

Date: _____

Draw a circle around the pictures and letter-symbols. Draw a line to match the pictures and letter-symbols. Say the sound for the letter-symbols as you draw the line.

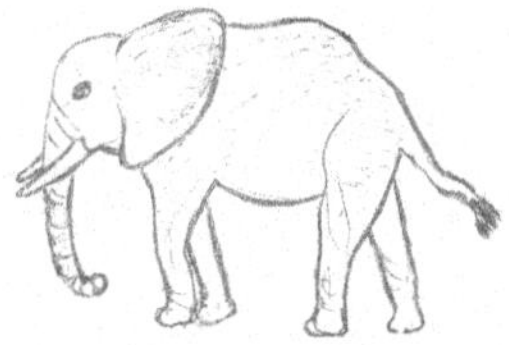

E   e

e   E

Name: _____

Date: _____

Color the picture of the **e**gg.

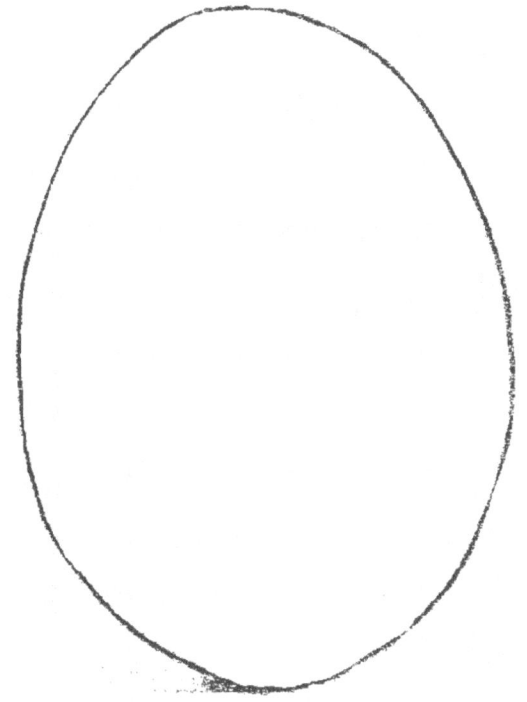

Say the words. Draw a line to the word that is the same.

egg   bed

beg   egg

bed   beg

w**e**b

Name: _____

Date: _____

Color the picture frame.
Trace the letter-symbols.
Say the sound.
Write the letter-symbols.

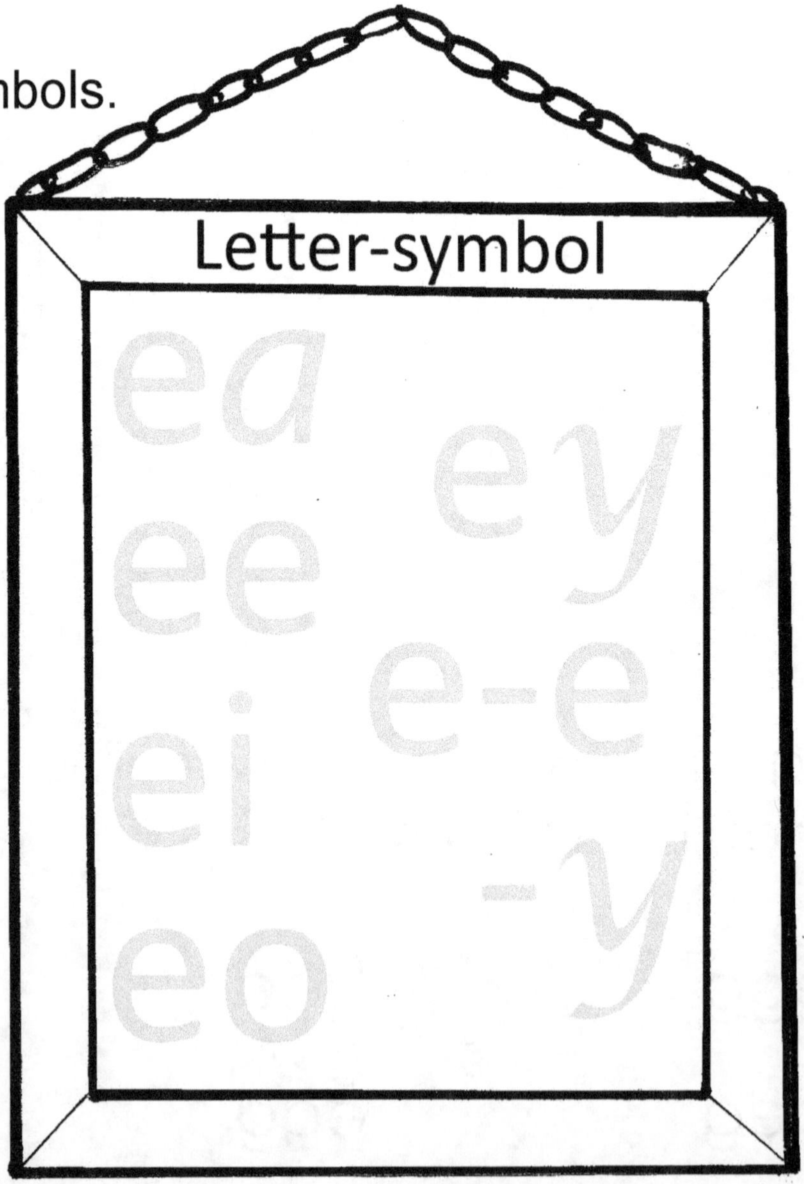

Letter-symbol

ea   ey
ee
ei   e-e
eo   -y

Page 35

Name: _____

Date: _____

Draw a circle around the pictures and letter-symbols. Draw a line to match the pictures and letter-symbols. Say the sound for the letter-symbols as you draw the line.

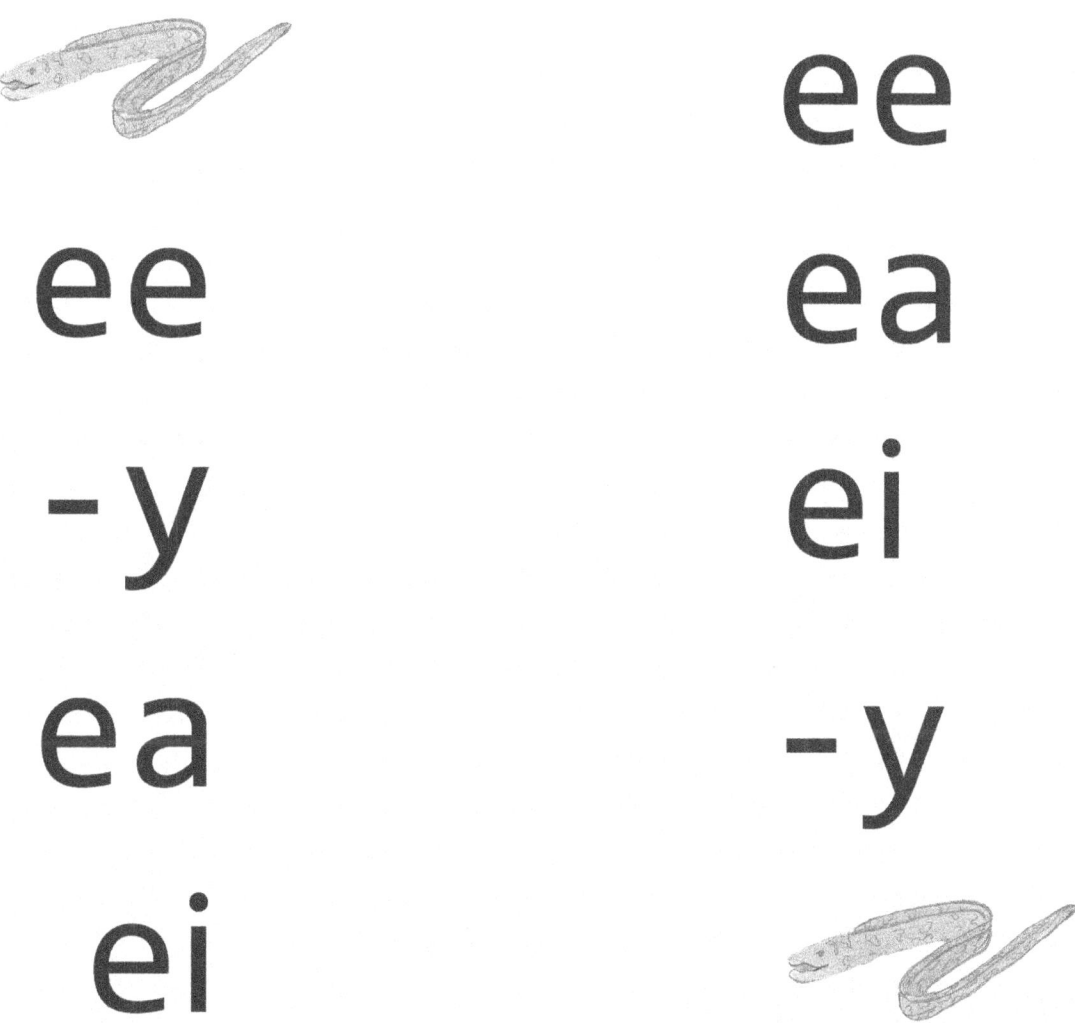

Name: _____

Date: _____

Color the picture of the **lea**f and the b**ee**.

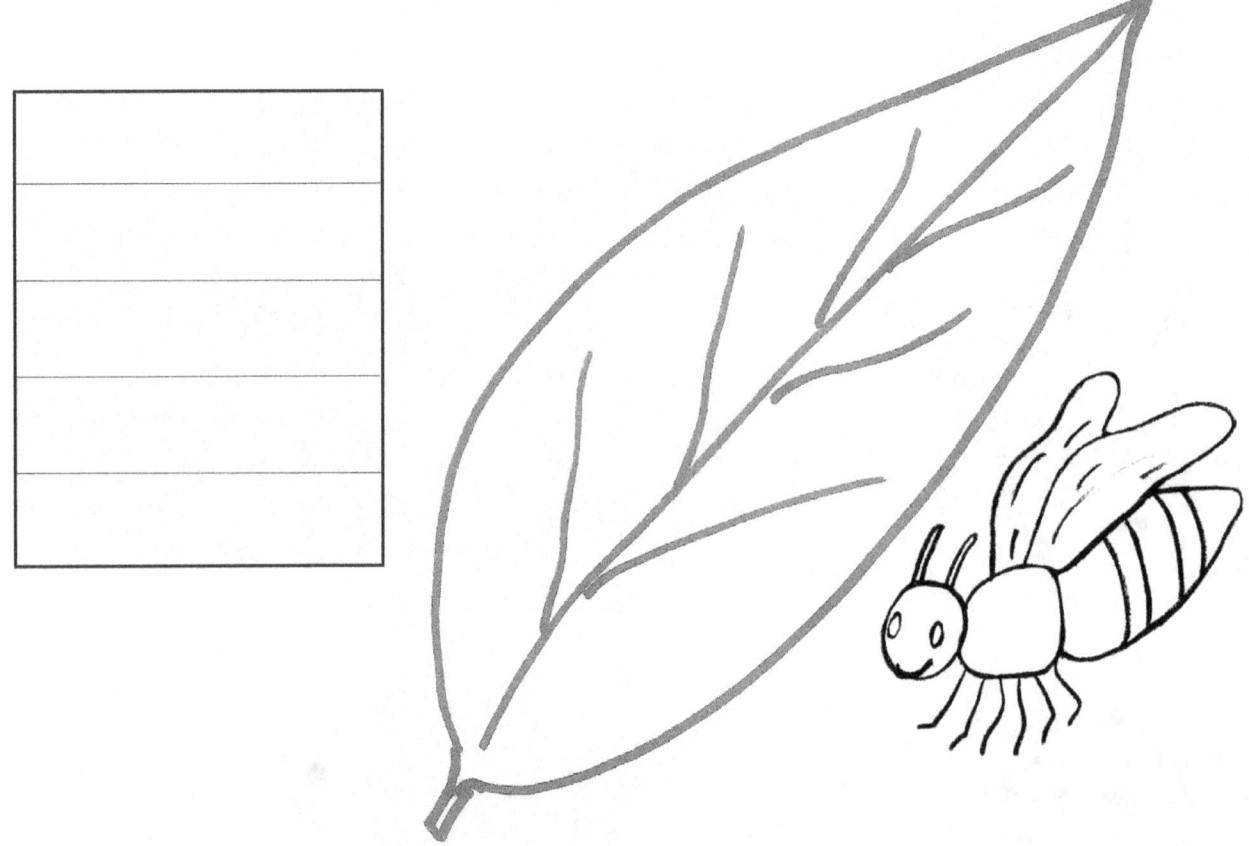

I see a leaf and a bee.
The leaf is green.
The bee has six legs.

Name: _____

Date: _____

Draw a circle around the pictures and letter-symbols. Draw a line to match the pictures and letter-symbols. Say the sound for the letter-symbols as you draw the line.

eo

ey

e-e

eo

ey

e-e

Tell the story "The Very Popular Mr. E".

Name: _____

Date: _____

Color the letter-symbols **eo ey e-e** yellow that are in the words.

people   key   these

Write these words

people   _____

key   _____

these   _____

Name:

Date:

Color the turk**ey**.

This is a turkey.

The turkey is a bird.

Name: _____

Date: _____

Color the picture frame.
Trace the letter-symbols.
Say the sound.
Write the letter-symbols.

Letter-symbol

ere

eer

Tell the story called "Triplets EER Celebrate".

Name: _____

Date: _____

Draw a circle around the pictures and letter-symbols. Draw a line to match the pictures and letter-symbols. Say the sound for the letter-symbols as you draw the line.

eer

eer

ere

ere

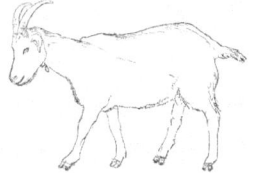

Name: _____

Date: _____

Color the picture of the d**eer**.

Find the letter-symbols **eer ere** in the words then color them yellow.

cheer   deer   here   where

Name: _____

Date: _____

Color the cashm**ere** goat.

This is a cashm**ere** goat.

It has soft hair.

It has four legs.

Name: _____

Date: _____

Color the picture frame.
Trace the letter-symbols.
Say the sound.
Write the letter-symbols.

Letter-symbol

er
ir
ur
ear-

Tell the story titled "This Is Her".

Name: _____

Date: _____

Draw a circle around the pictures and letter-symbols. Draw a line to match the pictures and letter-symbols. Say the sound for the letter-symbols as you draw the line.

ir

er

ur

ear-

er

ir

ear-

ur

Name: _____

Date: _____

Color the picture of the g**ir**l.

Match the words that are alike by drawing a line.

Say the words as you draw the line.

girl   sir

bird   dirt

sir   girl

dirt   bird

Now, color all the **ir** letter-symbols that you find in the words.

Name: _____

Date: _____

Circle the picture that is bigg**er**.
Draw an X on the picture that is small**er**.

b**ir**ds

g**ir**ls

goph**er**s

flow**er**s

Name: _____

Date: _____

Say the **er** sound for the letter-symbols.
Circle the picture in each row that has that sound in its name.

er	Her	Fish
ir	hare	girl
ur	turkey	dog

Name: _____

Date: _____

Color the ch**ur**ch.

Find the letter-symbol **ur** in the words and color it yellow.

turn   church   churn   burn

Name: _____

Date: _____

Color the picture frame.
Trace the letter-symbols.
Say the sound.
Write the letter-symbols.

Letter-symbol

-ar
-or
-er
-ure

Can you tell the story about the Bird Lady when she is tired?

Name: _____

Date: _____

Draw a circle around the pictures and letter-symbols. Draw a line to match the pictures and letter-symbols. Say the sound for the letter-symbols as you draw the line.

-ar	-ar
-or	-er
(picture)	-ure
-er	(picture)
-ure	-or

Copyright © 2021 Vinnette Mae Glidden — Pre-Reader Phonics — Page 52

Name: _____

Date: _____

Say a soft **er** sound for the letter-symbols.
Circle the picture in each row that has that sound.

--ar	calend**ar**	cat
--or	dog	col**or**
--ure	vult**ure**	bug

Name: _____

Date: _____

Use a soft **er** sound when you are reading the underlined letter-symbols in the story.

My broth<u>er</u> said he has a pict<u>ure</u> of an anch<u>or</u> and a pict<u>ure</u> of a vult<u>ure</u> in a ced<u>ar</u> tree.

Find the letter-symbols **ar or er ure** in the words below and color them light blue.

nectar

anchor

picture

sister

Name: _____

Date: _____

Color the picture frame.
Trace the letter-symbols.
Say the sound.
Write the letter-symbols.

uppercase
_____

lowercase
_____

lowercase
_____

Letter-symbol

F f

ph

Freddy and Fester are boxers. Can you tell the story about them?

Name: _____

Date: _____

Draw a circle around the pictures and letter-symbols. Draw a line to match the pictures and letter-symbols. Say the sound for the letter-symbols as you draw the line.

F			f

ph			F

f

ph

Name: _____

Date: _____

Color the ele**ph**ant.

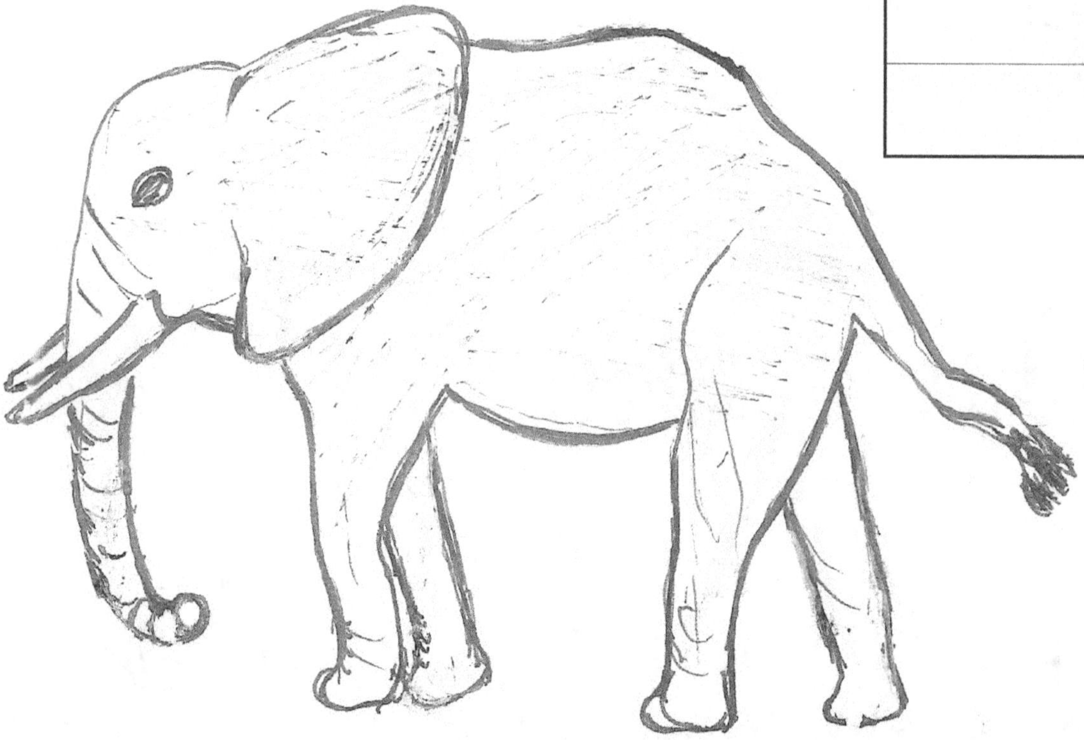

Color the letter-symbol **ph** in the words yellow.

phew   alpha   elephant   sphere

Name: _____

Date: _____

Color the **f**lag.

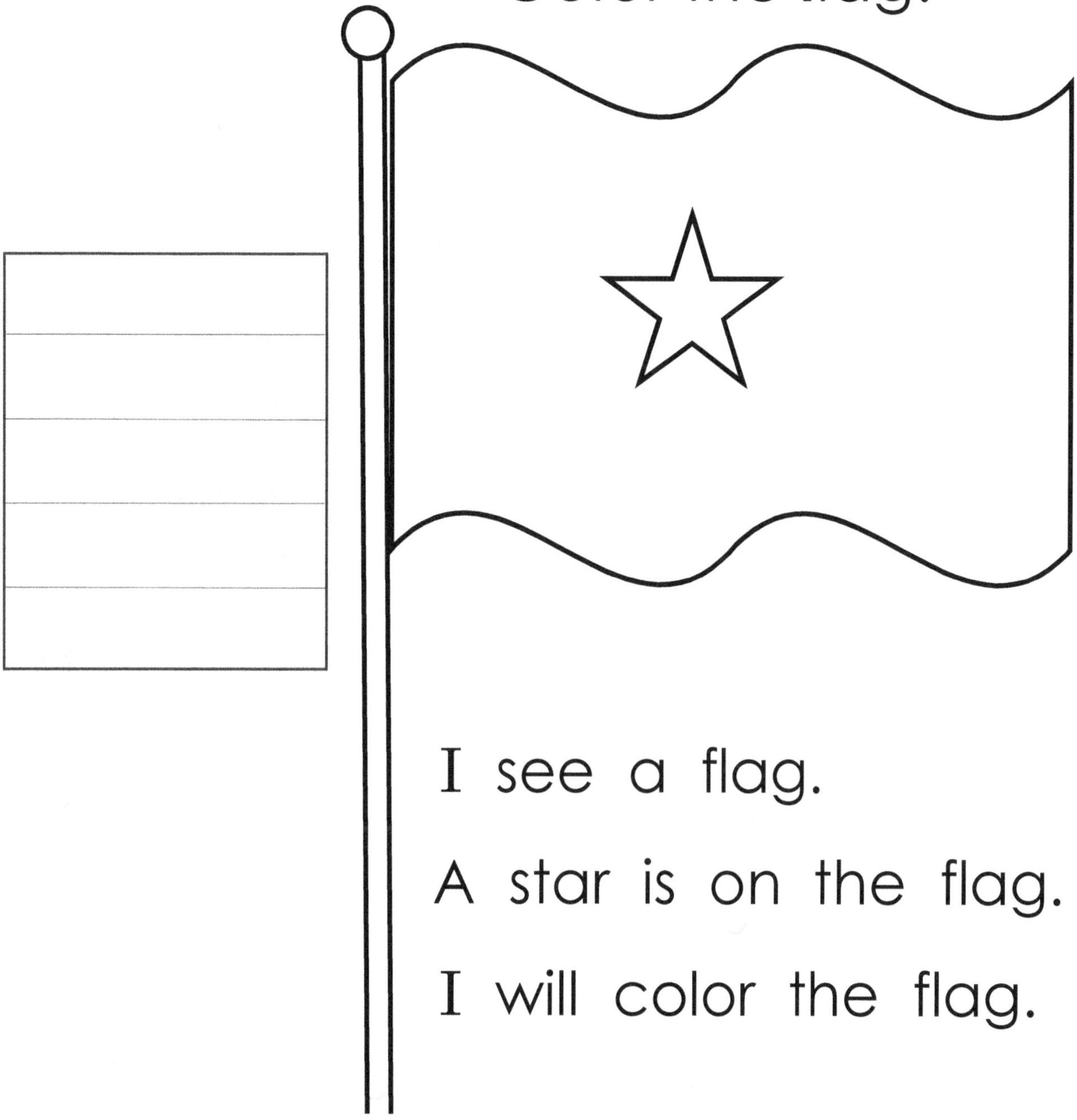

I see a flag.

A star is on the flag.

I will color the flag.

Name: _____

Date: _____

Color the picture frame.
Trace the letter-symbols.
Say the sound.
Write the letter-symbols.

uppercase G
_____

lowercase g
_____

Letter-symbol

gh-
G   g
-gue

Gatta g loves her baby Gabi. Gabi says /g/ /g/ /g/.

Name: _____

Date: _____

Draw a circle around the pictures and letter-symbols. Draw a line to match the pictures and letter-symbols. Say the sound for the letter-symbols as you draw the line.

gh-
G
g

-gue

G
-gue

gh-
g

Name: _____

Date: _____

Draw a picture on the bag.
Color the bag green.

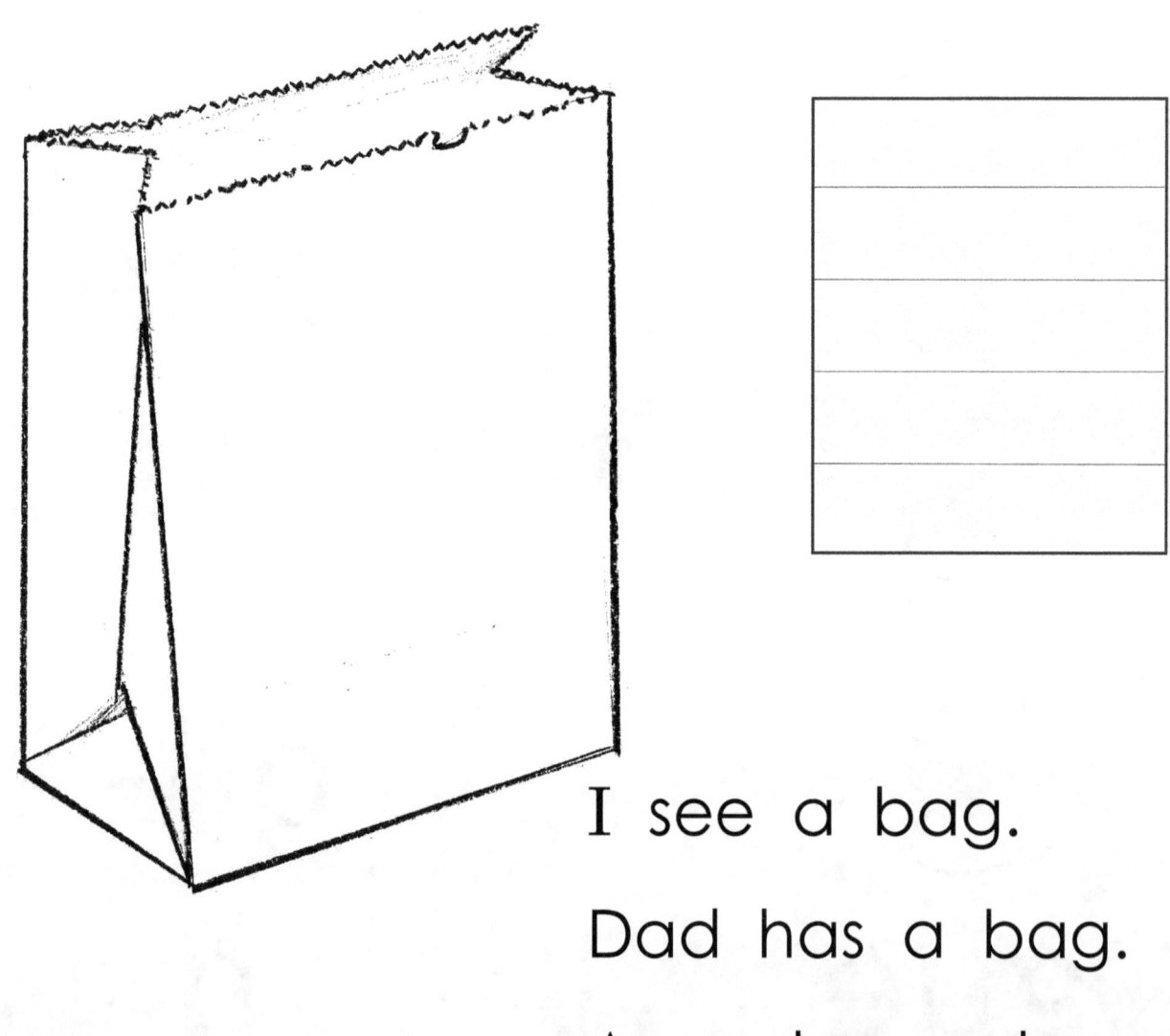

I see a bag.

Dad has a bag.

Anna has a bag.

Name: _____

Date: _____

Look at the pictures. Name the pictures. Find the letter-symbols **g gh G** in the name of the picture. Then color the letter-symbols **g gh G** pink.

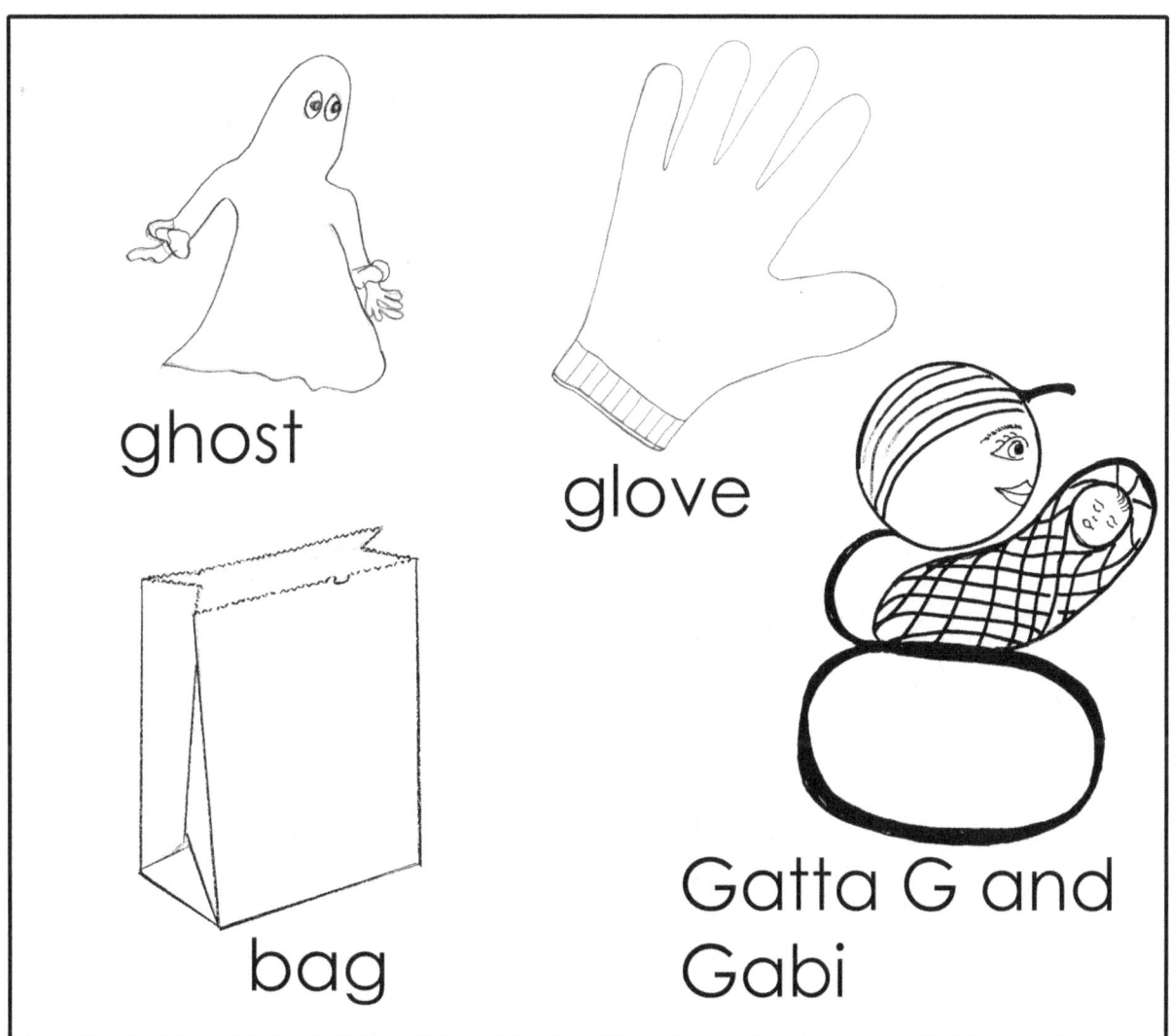

ghost

glove

bag

Gatta G and Gabi

Name: _____

Date: _____

Color the picture frame.
Trace the letter-symbols.
Say the sound.
Write the letter-symbols.

Letter-symbol

H
h

uppercase _____

lowercase _____

"Look out!" Harry h shouted. "Run!"
Tell the story about "Hilda's Bad Breath".

Name: _____

Date: _____

Draw a circle around the pictures and letter-symbols. Draw a line to match the pictures and letter-symbols. Say the sound for the letter-symbols as you draw the line.

H   h

h   H

Write uppercase H ___   Write lowercase h ___

Name: _____

Date: _____

Color the picture of the **h**ut.

I see a hut.
It is Dad's hut.
Can you see the hut?

Name: _____

Date: _____

Color the picture frame.
Trace the letter-symbols.
Say the sound.
Write the letter-symbols.

uppercase
_____
_____

lowercase
_____
_____

Letter-symbol

I

i

One night Aunt V had a dream. She saw a funny man.
Tell the story about "The Funny Man with Funny Eyes".

Name: ____________________

Date: ____________________

Draw a circle around the pictures and letter-symbols. Draw a line to match the pictures and letter-symbols. Say the sound for the letter-symbols as you draw the line.

I

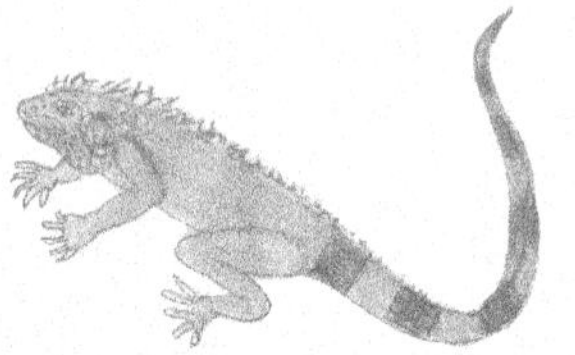

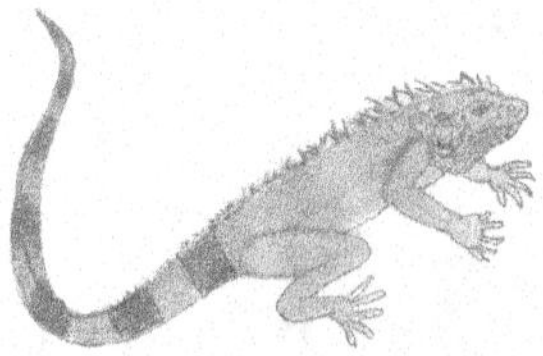

i

i

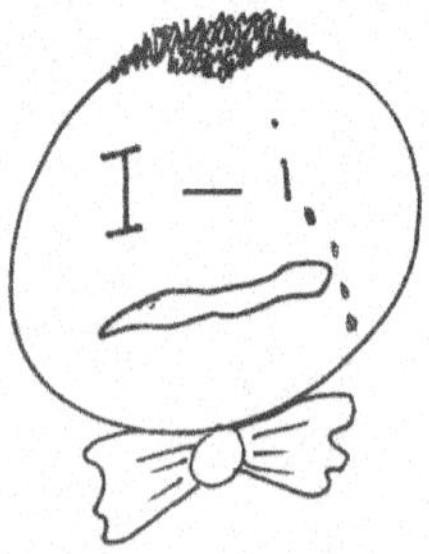

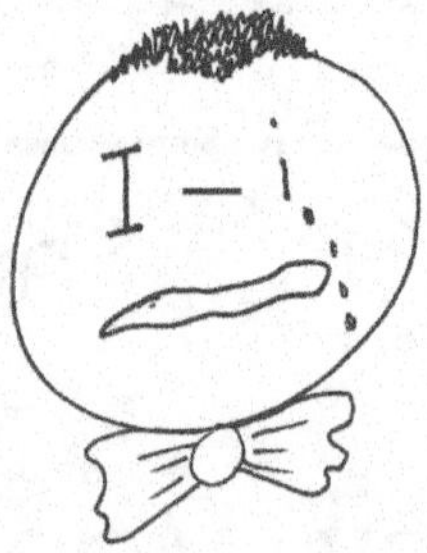

I

Name: _____

Date: _____

Color the picture.

This is the Funny Man.
He can cry.
He makes the sound i-i-i.

Name: _____

Date: _____

Color the picture frame.
Trace the letter-symbols.
Say the sound.
Write the letter-symbols.

Letter-symbol

I   ie   i-e   -y   igh

It is circus time! Allow me to introduce myself. Tell the "I-Man" story.

Name: _____

Date: _____

Draw a circle around the pictures and letter-symbols. Draw a line to match the pictures and letter-symbols. Say the sound for the letter-symbols as you draw the line.

Name: _____

Date: _____

Draw a circle around the pictures and letter-symbols. Draw a line to match the pictures and letter-symbols. Say the sound for the letter-symbols as you draw the line.

Name: _____

Date: _____

Say the sound for the letter-symbols. Circle the picture in each row that has that sound in its name.

Name: _____

Date: _____

Say the name of the pictures.
Write in the missing letter-symbols.
Color the picture.

sunl _ _ _ t

c r _

n _ _ _ tt _ m _

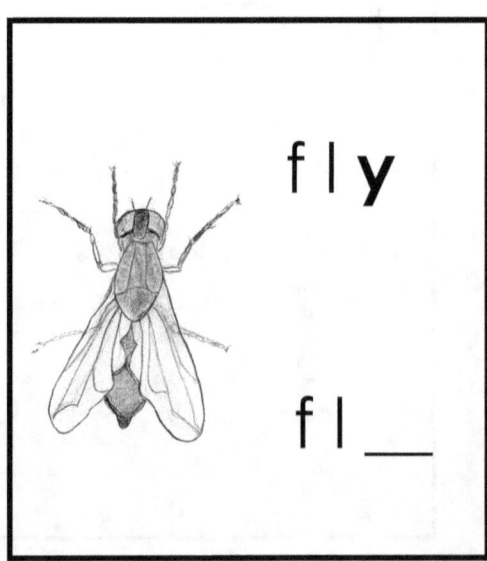

f l _

Name: _____

Date: _____

Color the pictures.

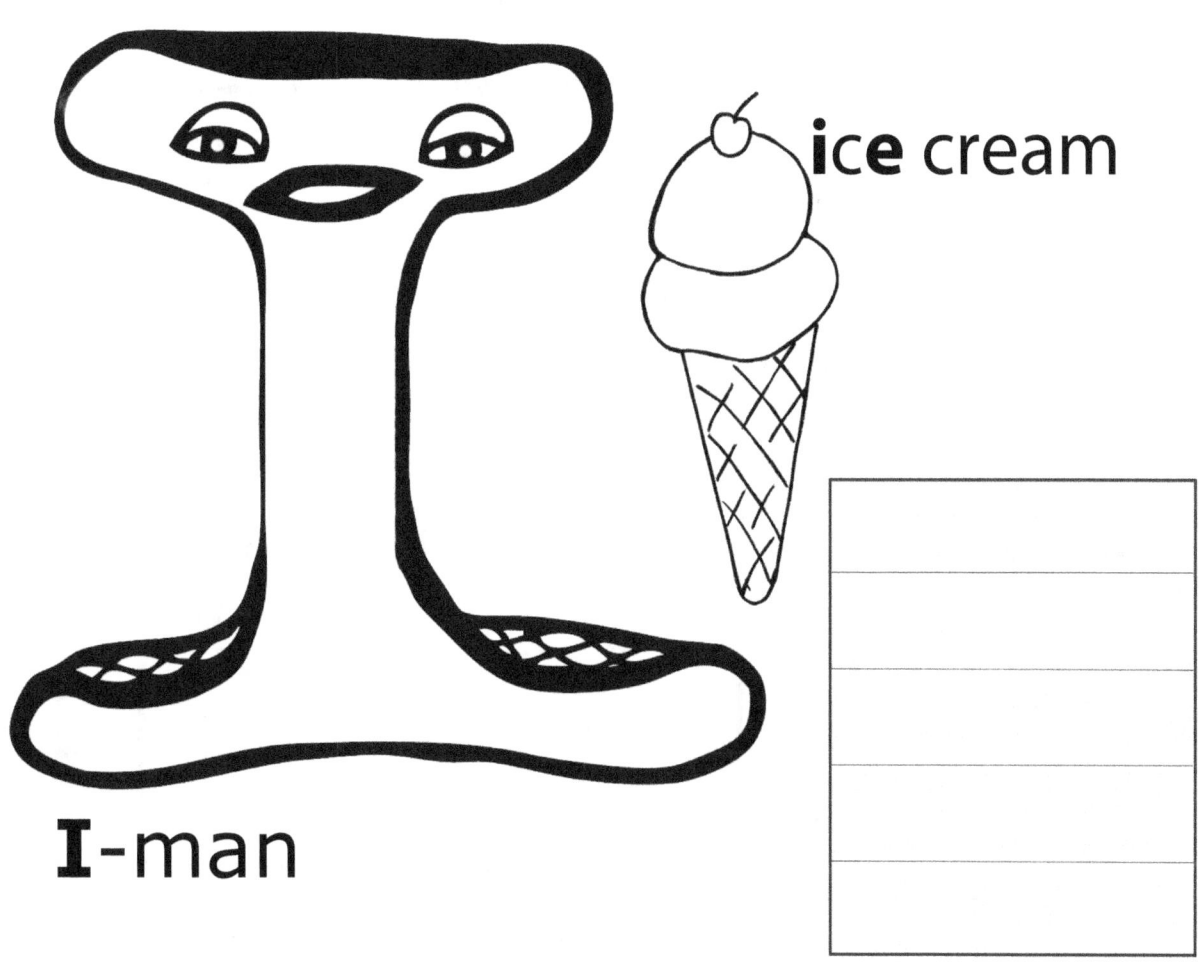

I-man

ice cream

I-man likes ice cream.
Anna likes ice cream.
Chad likes ice cream.

Date: _____

Color the picture frame.
Trace the letter-symbols.
Say the sound.
Write the letter-symbols.

uppercase J

lowercase j

Letter-symbol

J g e
j g i
   g y
  -dge

All the creatures and humans will hear Judge Gee's laws. Say the four laws in Judge Gee's court.

Name: _____

Date: _____

Draw a circle around the pictures and letter-symbols. Draw a line to match the pictures and letter-symbols. Say the sound for the letter-symbols as you draw the line.

J   j

j   J

Name: _____

Date: _____

Draw a circle around the pictures and letter-symbols. Draw a line to match the pictures and letter-symbols. Say the sound for the letter-symbols as you draw the line.

-dge

-dge

gy

gi

gi

gy

Name: _____

Date: _____

Color the letter-symbols **ge gi gy** in the words.

Match the letter-symbol with the correct word.

Ge   magic

gi   gym

gy   George

When the letter-symbol **g** has a **e i** or **y** after it, the **g** makes a /j/ sound.

Name: _____

Date: _____

Say the sound /j/ for the letter-symbols. Circle the picture in each row that has that sound in its name.

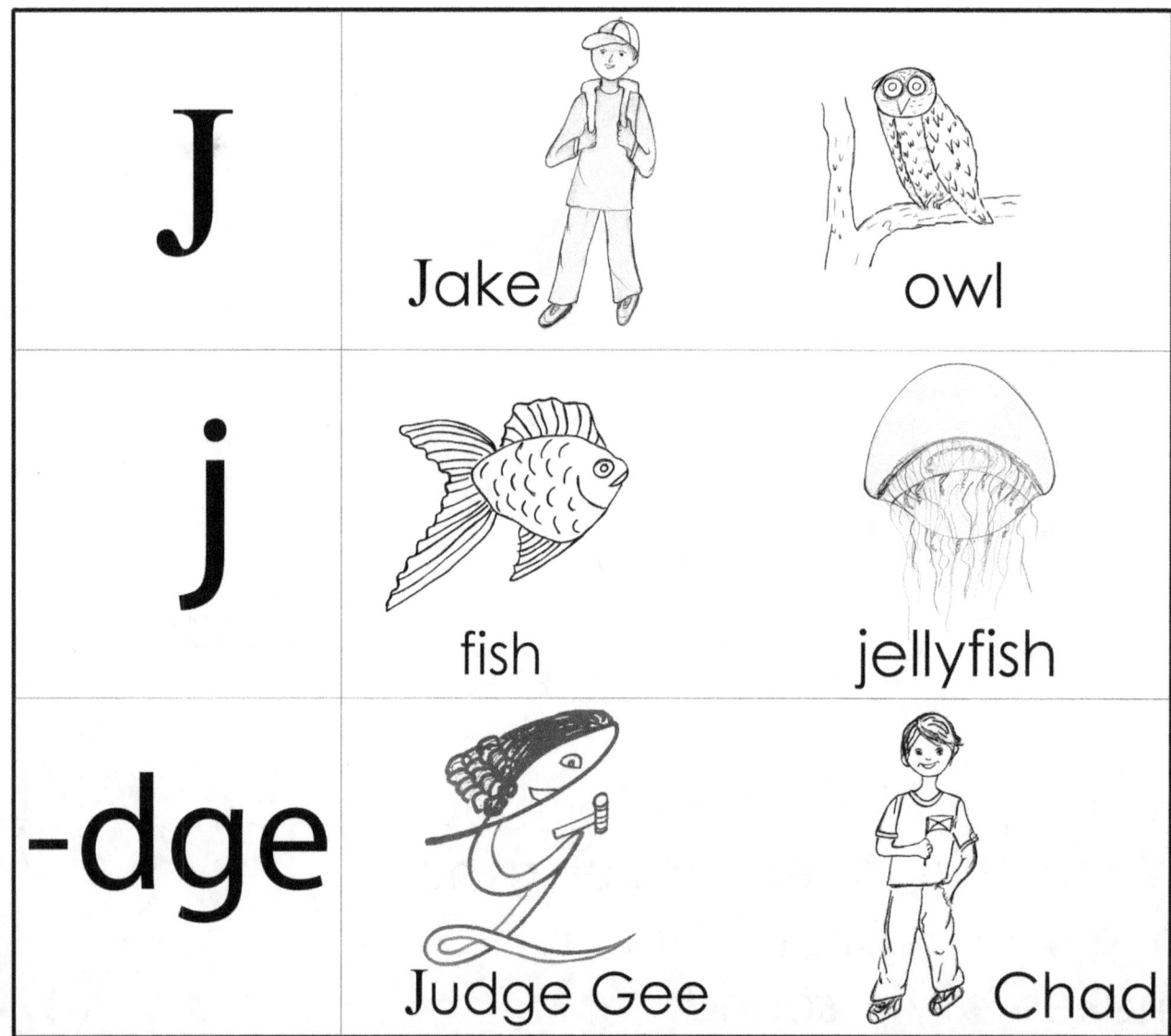

Name: _____

Date: _____

Color the ba**dge**.

I see a badge.
A star is on the badge.
The State Trooper has a badge.

Name: _____

Date: _____

Color the picture frame.
Trace the letter-symbols.
Say the sound.
Write the letter-symbols.

uppercase C

uppercase K

Letter-symbol

C -ck
k k
que

King K rules the kingdom in the Land of Make Believe. Tell the story "King K".

Name: _____

Date: _____

Draw a circle around the pictures and letter-symbols. Draw a line to match the pictures and letter-symbols. Say the sound for the letter-symbols as you draw the line.

-que

K

ck

K

-que

ck

Name: _____

Date: _____

Color the **k**ite.

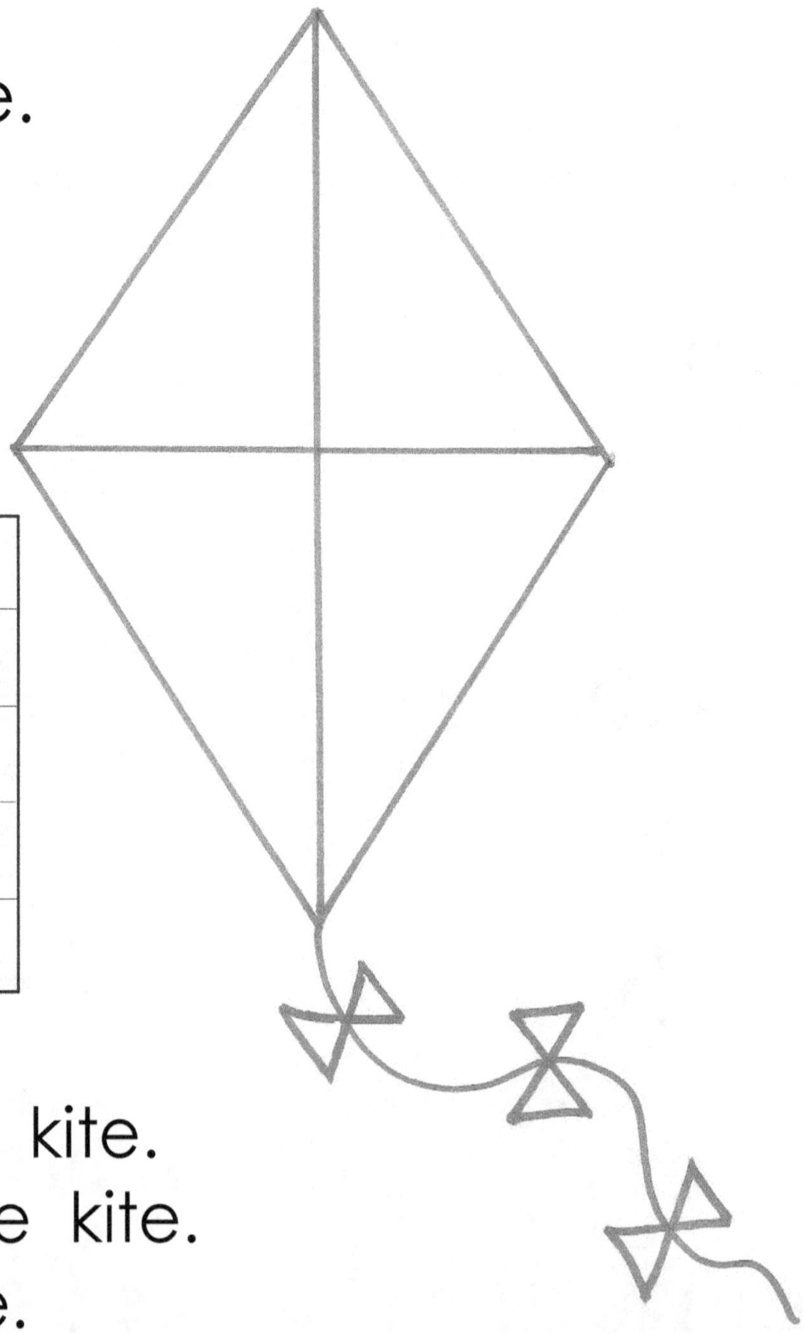

King K has a kite.
I can see the kite.
I like the kite.
The kite has a tail.

Name: _____

Date: _____

Say the sound **/k/** for the letter-symbols.
Circle the picture in each row that has that sound in its name.

Name: _____

Date: _____

Can you find these letter-symbols **K k c** in these words? Color them yellow.

Ken					jackel

bike					book

back					cake

Draw a picture

Name: _____

Date: _____

Color the ja**ck**al.

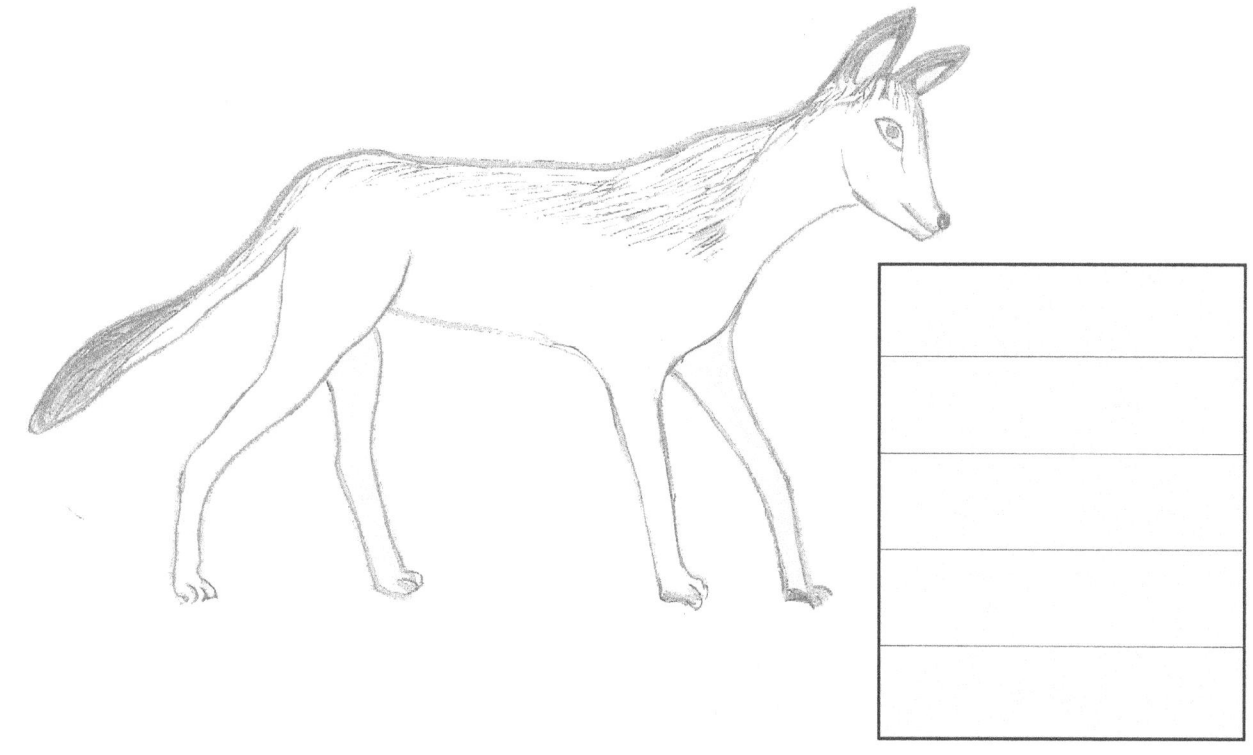

This is a jackal.
The jackal looks like a dog.
I saw a big jackal in my book.
The jackal runs fast.

Name: _____

Date: _____

Color the picture frame.
Trace the letter-symbols.
Say the sound /**kw**/ for **qu**.
Write the letter-symbols.

Letter-symbol

Qu
qu

uppercase Qu
_____

lowercase qu
_____

Queen Q is the most beautiful woman.
U-vowel is always by her side.
Tell the story "Queen Q and Her Guard".

Name: _____

Date: _____

Draw a circle around the pictures and letter-symbols. Draw a line to match the pictures and letter-symbols. Say the sound for the letter-symbols as you draw the line.

qu   Qu

Qu

                      qu

Name: _____

Date: _____

Color the picture.

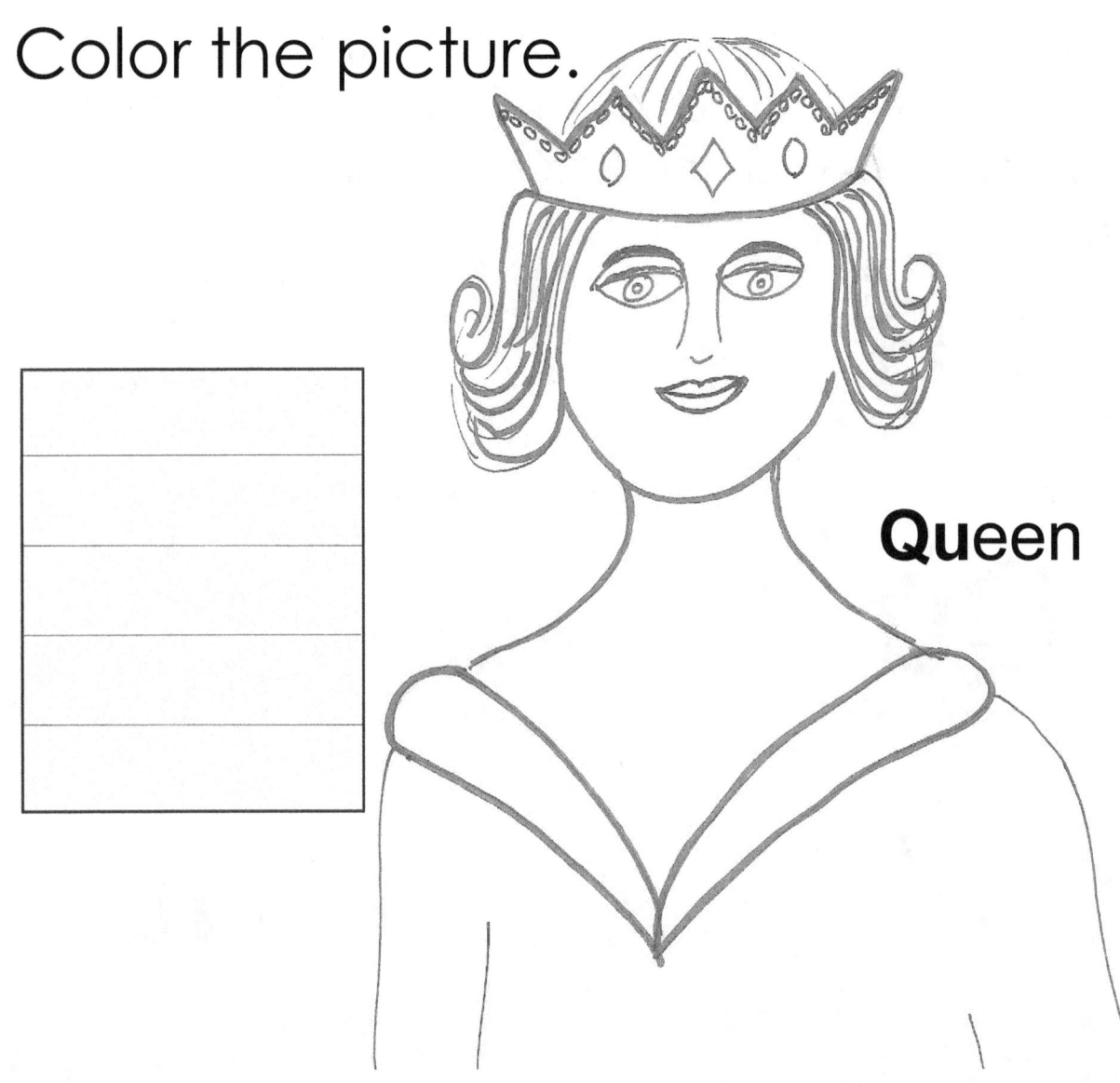

Queen

This is a queen.
A queen sits on a throne.
The queen has a crown.

Name: _____

Date: _____

Color the picture of the **qu**ail.

A quail is a bird.
This is a quail.
It has a short tail.
Queen Q likes the quail.

Name:

Date:

Color the picture frame.
Trace the letter-symbols.
Say the sounds /**ks**/ for **x**.
/**gz**/ for **x**
Write the letter-symbol.

Letter-symbol

uppercase X

lowercase x

X marks the spot on the big box.
Mr. X says **X** is equal to **ks**.
Mr. X says **X** is equal to **cks**.
Mr. X says **X** is equal to **gz**.

Name: _____

Date: _____

Draw a circle around the pictures and letter-symbols. Draw a line to match the pictures and letter-symbols. Say the sound for the letter-symbols as you draw the line.

Find the letter-symbol X in the words and color it pink.

box   fox   taxi   Max

Name: _____

Date: _____

Color the pictures.

I see a fox.
The fox has a tail.
The fox has four legs.

Name: _____

Date: _____

Color the picture frame.
Trace the letter-symbols.
Say the sound.
Write the letter-symbols.

uppercase L
_____
_____

lowercase l
_____
_____

lowercase le
_____
_____

Letter-symbol

L l
-le

"Lee Lee Makes Me Laugh".
Lee Lee is tall and happy.
Tell Lee Lee's story.

Name:

Date:

Draw a circle around the pictures and letter-symbols. Draw a line to match the pictures and letter-symbols. Say the sound for the letter-symbols as you draw the line.

L L

l 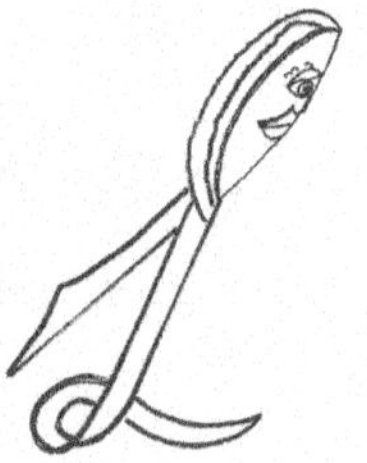

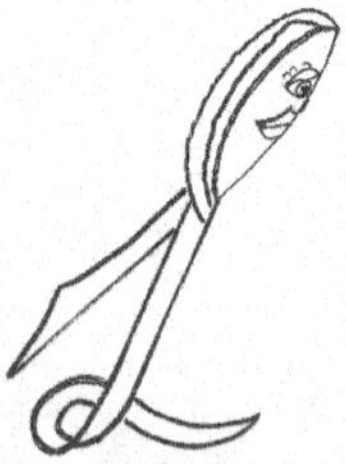 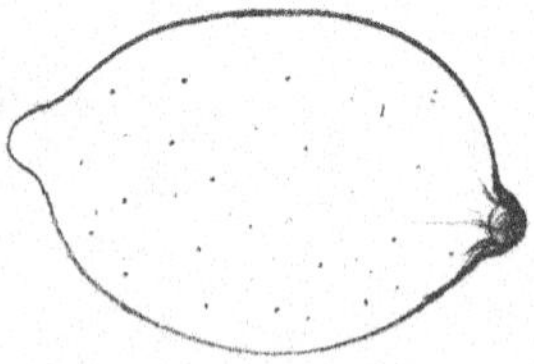

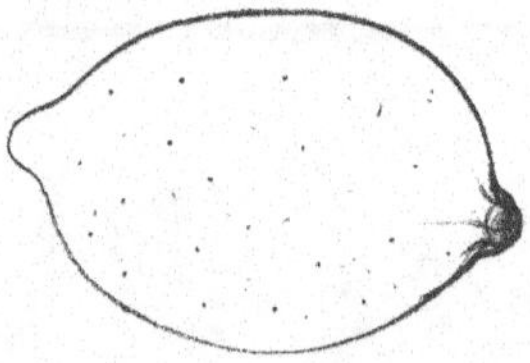 l

Name: _____

Date: _____

Color this lemon yellow.

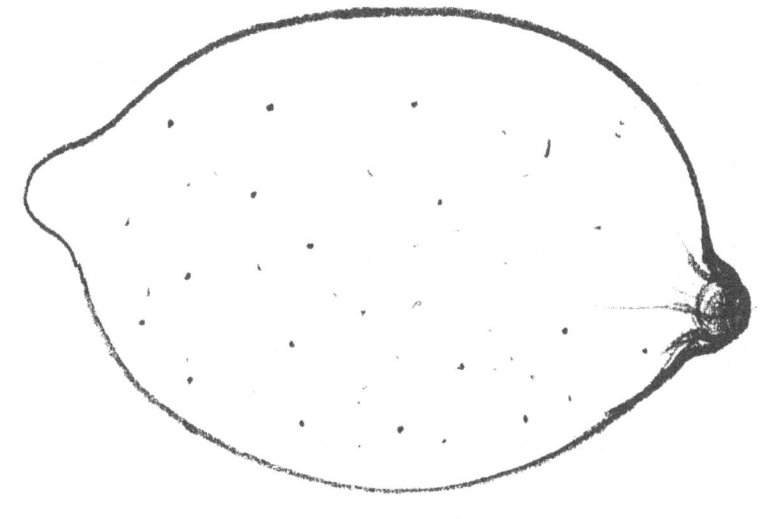

I can see it.
It is big.
It is a big yellow lemon.

Name:

Date:

Color the picture frame.
Trace the letter-symbols.
Say the sound.
Write the letter-symbols.

uppercase M

lowercase m

Letter-symbol

-mn
M m
-mb

Emma and Meme eat the mango candies, rub their tummies and say mmm...
Can you tell the story "Emma and the Candy Jar"?

Name: _____

Date: _____

Draw a circle around the pictures and letter-symbols. Draw a line to match the pictures and letter-symbols. Say the sound for the letter-symbols as you draw the line.

-mn

M

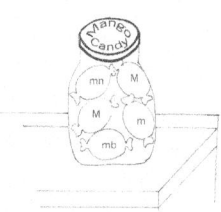

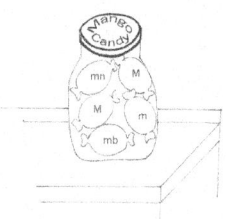

-mn

M

Name: _____

Date: _____

Color the picture of the **m**oon.

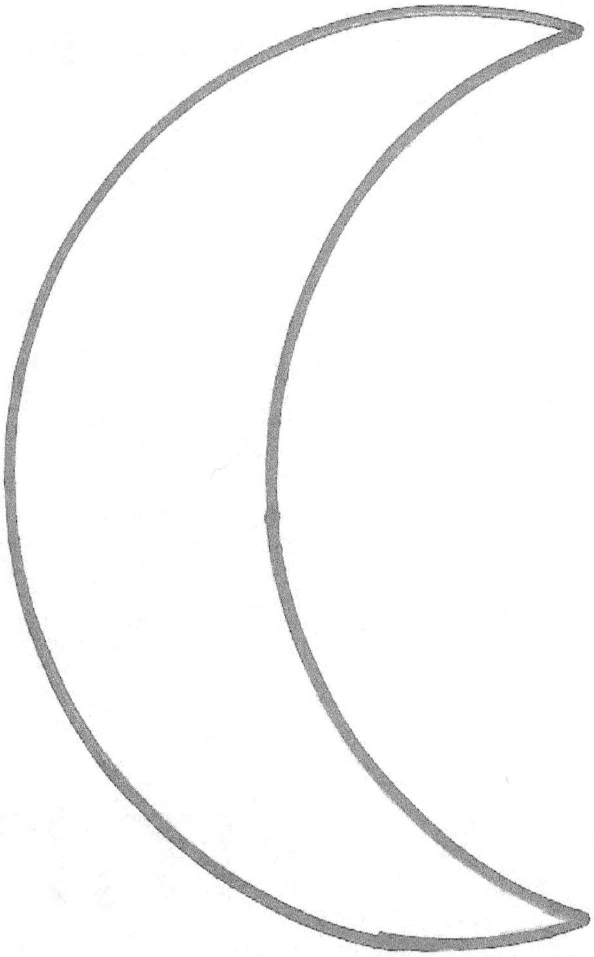

I see the moon.
I see the moon at night.
Can you see the moon?_____

Name: _____

Date: _____

Draw a circle around the pictures and letter-symbols. Draw a line to match the pictures and letter-symbols. Say the sound for the letter-symbols as you draw the line.

Name: _____

Date: _____

Say the sound **/m/** for the letter-symbols.
Circle the picture in each row that has that sound in its name.

Name: _____

Date: _____

Color the picture frame.
Trace the letter-symbols.
Say the sound.
Write the letter-symbols.

uppercase N

lowercase n

Letter-symbol

N n kn- gn

"Watch me write the letter-symbols on my knee," said Nightingale.
Tell the story called "Norma and Nightingale".

Name: _____

Date: _____

Draw a circle around the pictures and letter-symbols.
Draw a line to match the pictures and letter-symbols.
Say the sound for the letter-symbols as you draw the line.

Kn

n

n

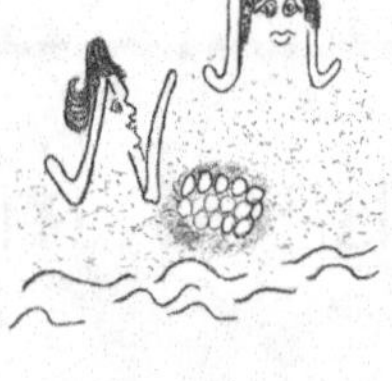

Kn

Name: _____

Date: _____

Say the sound **/n/** for the letter-symbols.
Circle the picture in each row that has that sound in its name.

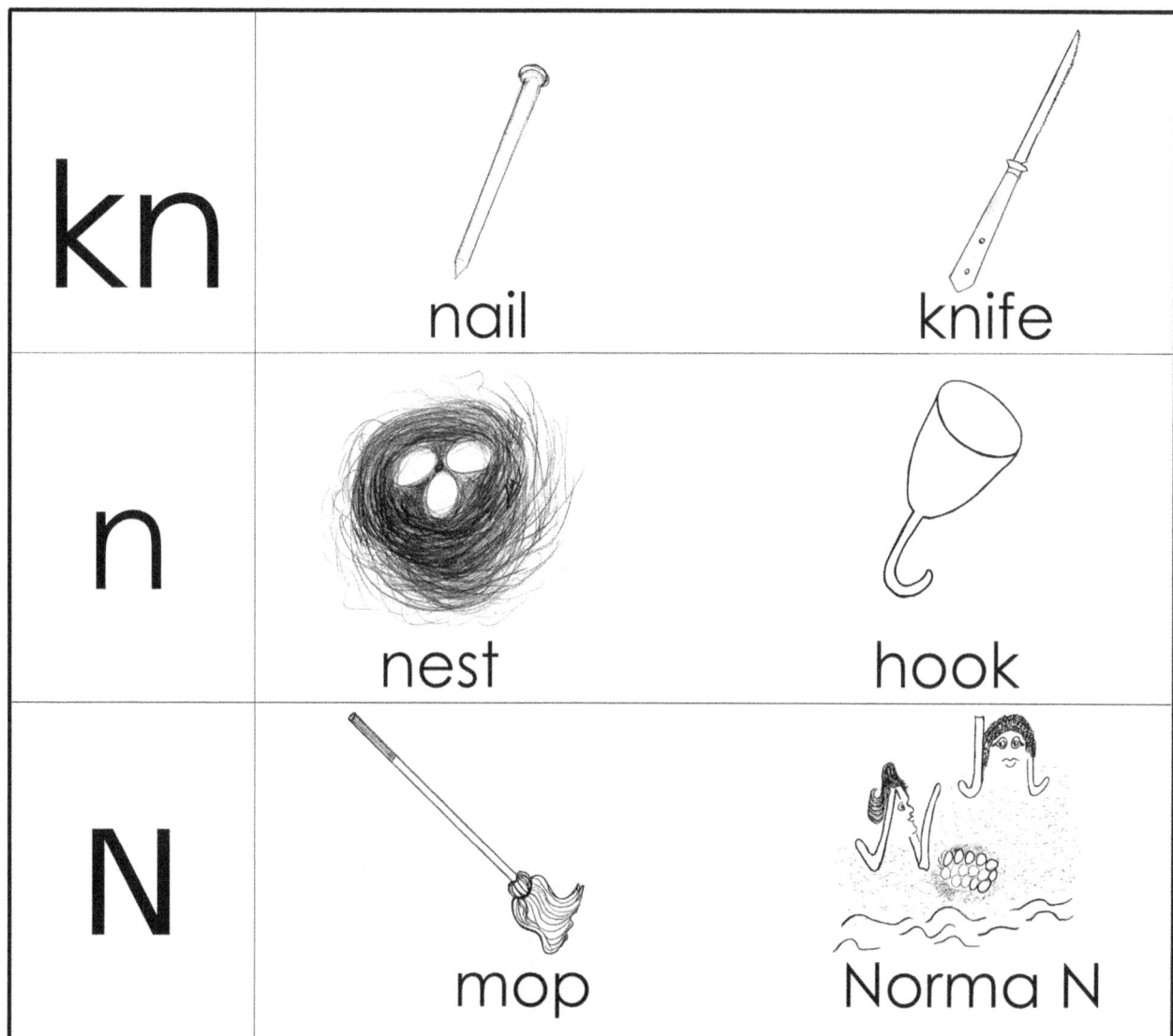

Name: _____

Date: _____

Color the picture of **n**umber **nin**e.

This is number nine.
Make nine circles _____
Norma has nine beds.
Queen Q has nine quails and I have nine pencils.

Date: _____

Color the picture frame.
Trace the letter-symbols.
Say the sounds.
Write the letter-symbols.

Letter-symbol

-ng
k
-n
c
-n
x
-ng
g-

Norma N spends lots of time learning to make sounds. Tell the story "Norma and Gee".

Name: _____

Date: _____

Draw a circle around the pictures and letter-symbols. Draw a line to match the pictures and letter-symbols. Say the sound for the letter-symbols as you draw the line.

-ng

-nk

-nk

-ng

Name: _____

Date: _____

Color the picture of the wi**ng**s.

ink

I see two wings.
A bird has two wings.
A bird needs two wings to fly.

Name: _____

Date: _____

Color the picture frame.
Trace the letter-symbols.
Say the sound.
Write the letter-symbol.

uppercase O
_____

lowercase o
_____

Letter-symbol

O

If you put an O in your hand then gently tap your forehead and make the short o-vowel sound you will remember the sound and symbol.
Tell the story "The Hand With the O".

Name: _____

Date: _____

Draw a circle around the pictures and letter-symbols. Draw a line to match the pictures and letter-symbols. Say the sound for the letter-symbols as you draw the line.

O-

O-

Find the letter-symbol O in each word and color it light green.

on   dot   job   hot

Name: _____

Date: _____

Color the picture of the **o**ctopus.

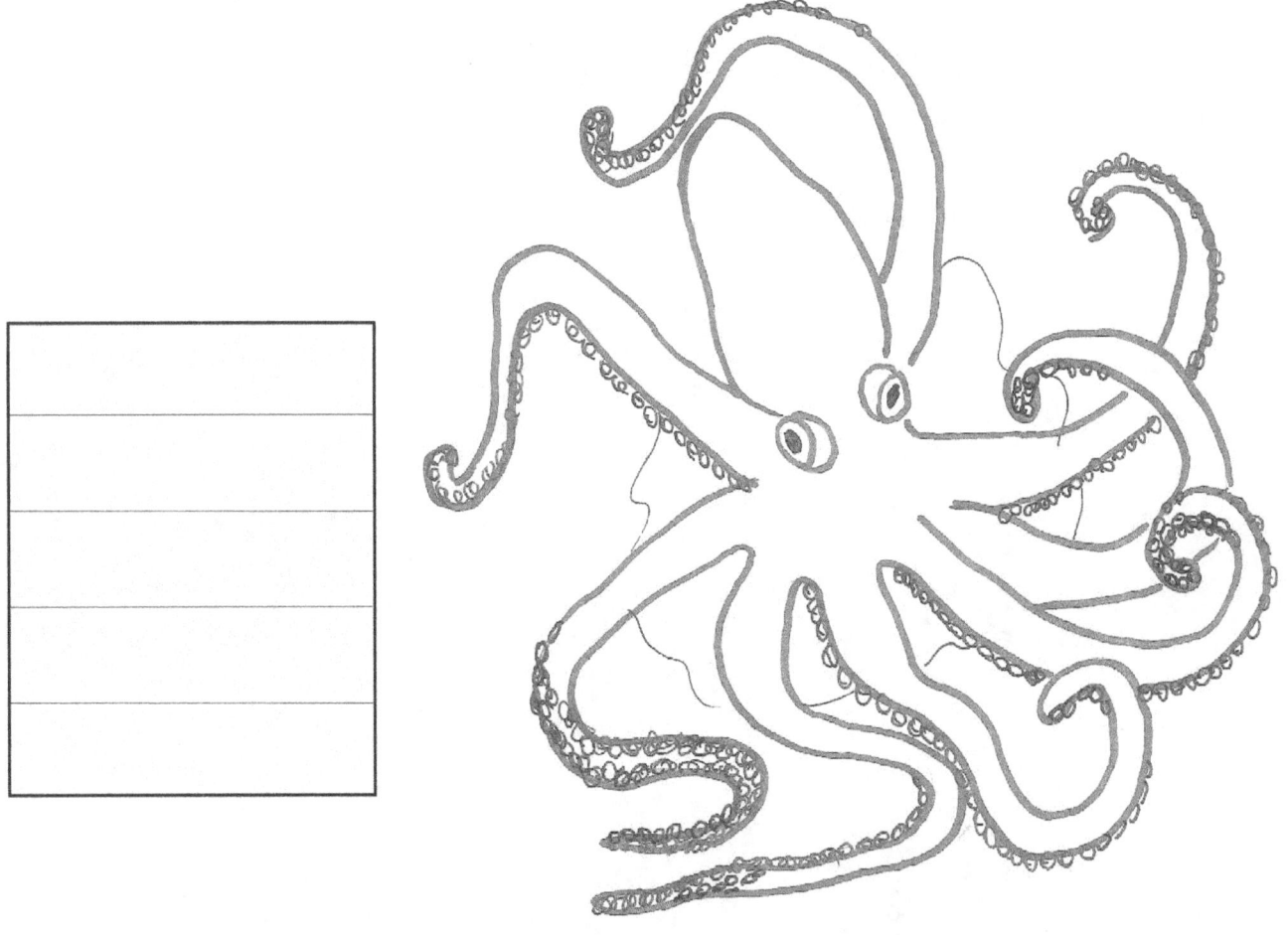

I see an octopus.
An octopus has eight legs.
It is in the sea.
It is big.

Name: _____

Date: _____

Color the picture of the hand.

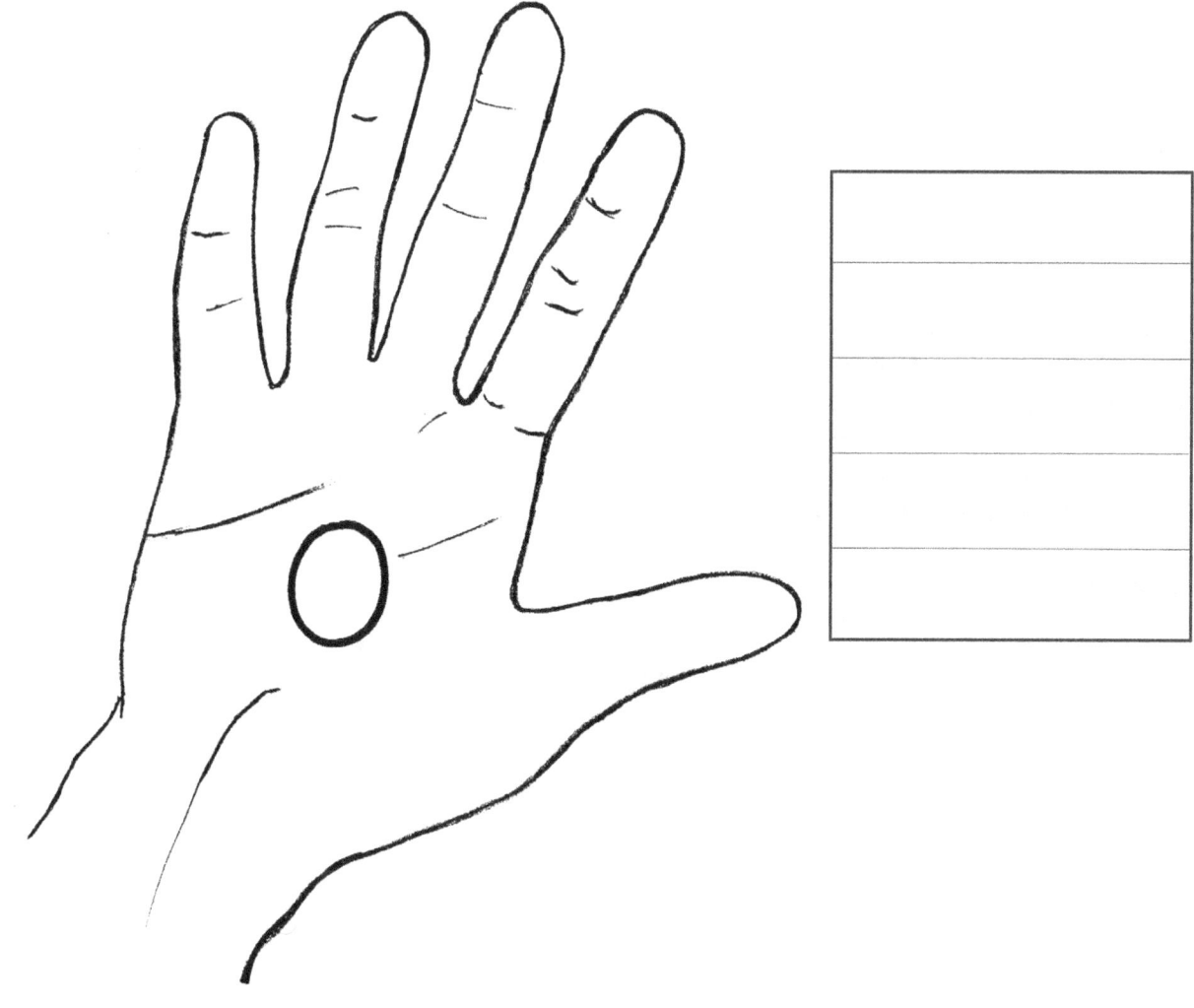

This hand has an O.
I can make the O sound, can you?

Name: _____

Date: _____

Oh! The Beautiful Roses

Color the picture.

Name: _____

Date: _____

Color the picture frame.
Trace the letter-symbols.
Say the sound.
Write the letter-symbols.

Letter-symbol

oa
oe
o-e
-o -ow

"Just look at that long conga line," shouted Joe. Tell the story "Oh! The Beautiful Roses".

Name: _____

Date: _____

Draw a circle around the pictures and letter-symbols. Draw a line to match the pictures and letter-symbols. Say the sound for the letter-symbols as you draw the line.

oa   -o

oe

-o   oa

oe

Name: _____

Date: _____

1. Color the sea blue.
2. Put four stars on the sail.
3. Do not color the sail.
4. Color the boat red.

B**oa**t

Dad has a boat.
Dad took me on the boat.
The boat has a sail.

Name: _____

Date: _____

Draw a circle around the pictures and letter-symbols. Draw a line to match the pictures and letter-symbols. Say the sound for the letter-symbols as you draw the line.

o-e   -ow

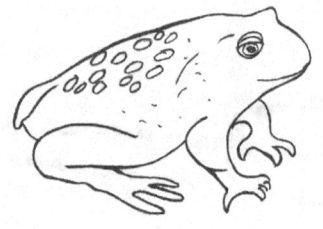

o-e

-ow

Find the letter-symbols **oa**, **ow**, **o-e** in the words. Color them light green.
snow   yellow   toad   boat

Name: _____

Date: _____

Color **Toa**d yellow.
How many spots are on **Toa**d? _____

This is Toad.
I can see Toad.
Toad has lots of bumps.
Toad has four legs.
Toad can jump high.

Name: _____

Date: _____

Color the picture frame.
Trace the letter-symbols.
Say the sound.
Write the letter-symbol.

Letter-symbol

or

Everything O-Vowel and R-Consonant have in their stall begins with **or**.
Tell the story about "O and R's Stall".

Name: _____

Date: _____

Draw a circle around the pictures and letter-symbols. Draw a line to match the pictures and letter-symbols. Say the sound for the letter-symbols as you draw the line.

Look at the words and color the letter-symbols **or** yellow.

corn   horn   organ   horse

Name: _____

Date: _____

Color the h**or**se brown.

I see a horse.
The horse neighs.
The horse has a long tail and a big nose.

Name: _____

Date: _____

Color the picture frame.
Trace the letter-symbols.
Say the sound.
Write the letter-symbols.

Letter-symbol

ou
ow
ough

Tell the story "Ou Ow Not Today".

Name: _____

Date: _____

Draw a circle around the pictures and letter-symbols. Draw a line to match the pictures and letter-symbols. Say the sound for the letter-symbols as you draw the line.

ou   ow

ow

   ou

Name: _____

Date: _____

Color the cl**ow**n.

Match the words that are the same.

clown   brown

town   clown

brown   town

This is a clown.
He goes around the town.
His name is Mr. Brown.

Name:

Date:

Color the picture of the h**ou**se.

This house is small.
Mom has a big house.
Anna has a small house.

Name: _____

Date: _____

Color the picture of the **cow**.

I see Betty the cow.
She has four legs.
She has a long tail.
Betty says moo.

Name: _____

Date: _____

Color the picture frame.
Trace the letter-symbols.
Say the sound.
Write the letter-symbols.

Letter-symbol

oo
ui
-u

Suddenly, they heard **oo**, **oo**, **oo**.
"It's me U-Vowel and I-man Sir."
Tell the story "OO OO Said the Owl".

Name: _____

Date: _____

Draw a circle around the pictures and letter-symbols. Draw a line to match the pictures and letter-symbols. Say the sound for the letter-symbols as you draw the line.

oo

ui

-u

-u

oo

ui

Name: _____

Date: _____

Color the picture of the ball**oo**ns.

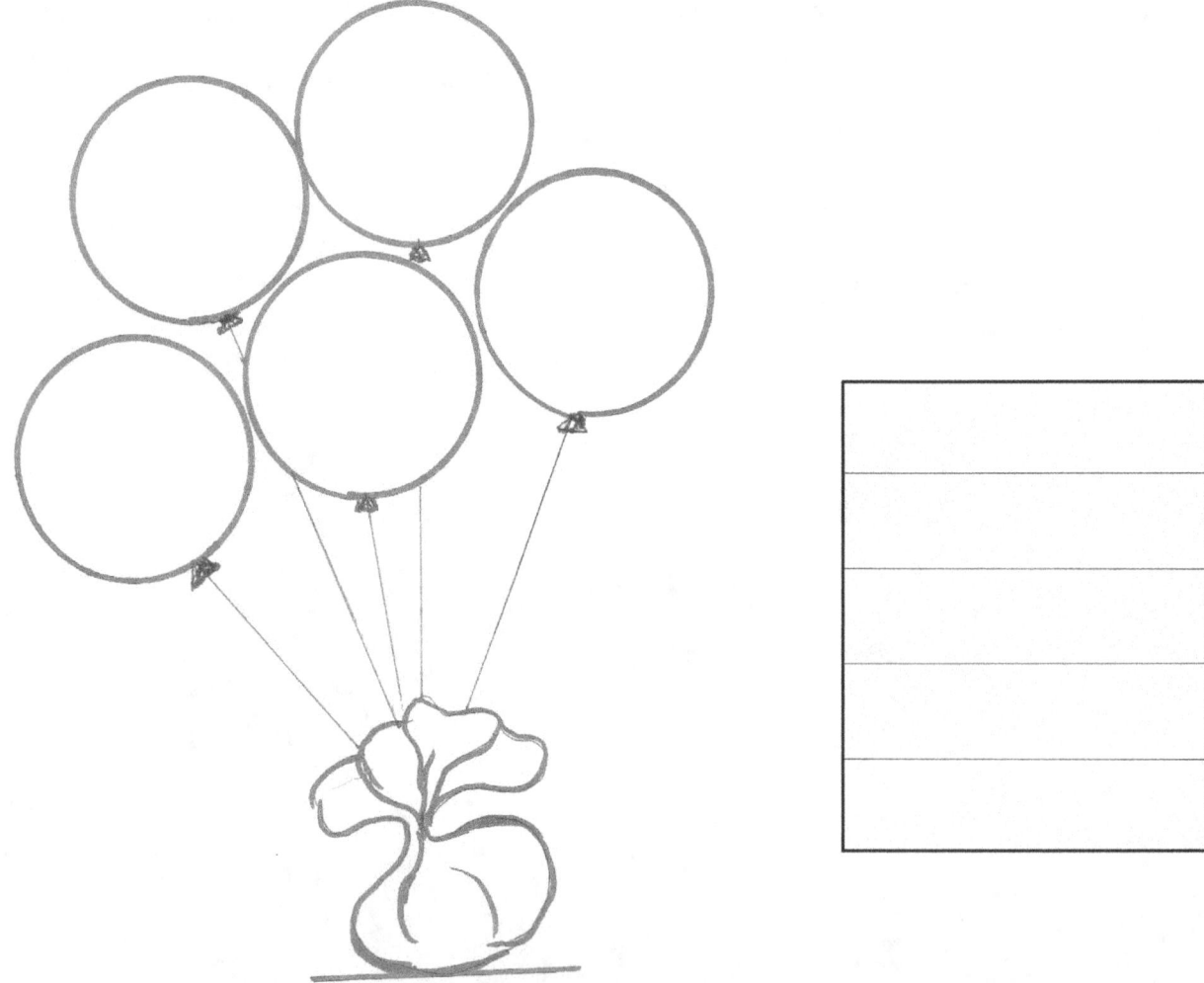

I see five balloons.
Mom and Dad got five balloons.
Anna and Chad like the balloons.

Name:

Date:

Color the fr**ui**ts.

I see an apple.
I see a banana.
I see two fruits.
I can eat them.

Name: _____

Date: _____

Color the picture frame.
Trace the letter-symbols.
Say the sound **oo**.
Write the letter-symbols.

Letter-symbol

ook
ood
ull

Mr. U-Vowel and I-man burst through the door. Tell the story "Happy to be Home **ook**".

Name: _____

Date: _____

Draw a circle around the pictures and letter-symbols. Draw a line to match the pictures and letter-symbols. Say the sound for the letter-symbols as you draw the line.

ook

ook

ull

ull

Name: _____

Date: _____

Make the sound /oo/ as in b**oo**.
Now, color the **oo** letter-symbol yellow in the names of the pictures. Read the words.

hood   hook

Make the sound for the **u** letter-symbol in the words f**u**ll and p**u**ll.
Now, color the **u** letter-symbol yellow in the names of the pictures. Read the words.

full   pull

Name: _____

Date: _____

Color the picture frame.
Trace the letter-symbols.
Say the sound.
Write the letter-symbols.

Letter-symbol

oi
oy

"Oi! Oi! Oy! Guys you scared the jumbies out of me," screamed Aunt V.
Tell the "Oi! Oi! Oy! Cried Aunt V" story.

Name: _____

Date: _____

Draw a circle around the pictures and letter-symbols. Draw a line to match the pictures and letter-symbols. Say the sound for the letter-symbols as you draw the line.

oi

oy

oy

oi

Name: _____

Date: _____

Color the picture.

This boy has a toy truck.
He pulls it with a string.
He likes his toy truck.
Do you have a pull toy?

Name: _____

Date: _____

Color the picture frame.
Trace the letter-symbols.
Say the sound.
Write the letter-symbols.

uppercase P
_____
_____

lowercase p
_____
_____

Letter-symbol

P
p

It sounds like a slight explosion.
Tell the "Nobody Likes to Sit by Mr. P" story.

Name: _____

Date: _____

Draw a circle around the pictures and letter-symbols. Draw a line to match the pictures and letter-symbols. Say the sound for the letter-symbols as you draw the line.

Find the **P** letter-symbol in the words and color the **P** yellow.

pop　　cap　　mop　　pet

Name: _____

Date: _____

Color the picture of the **p**um**p**kin.

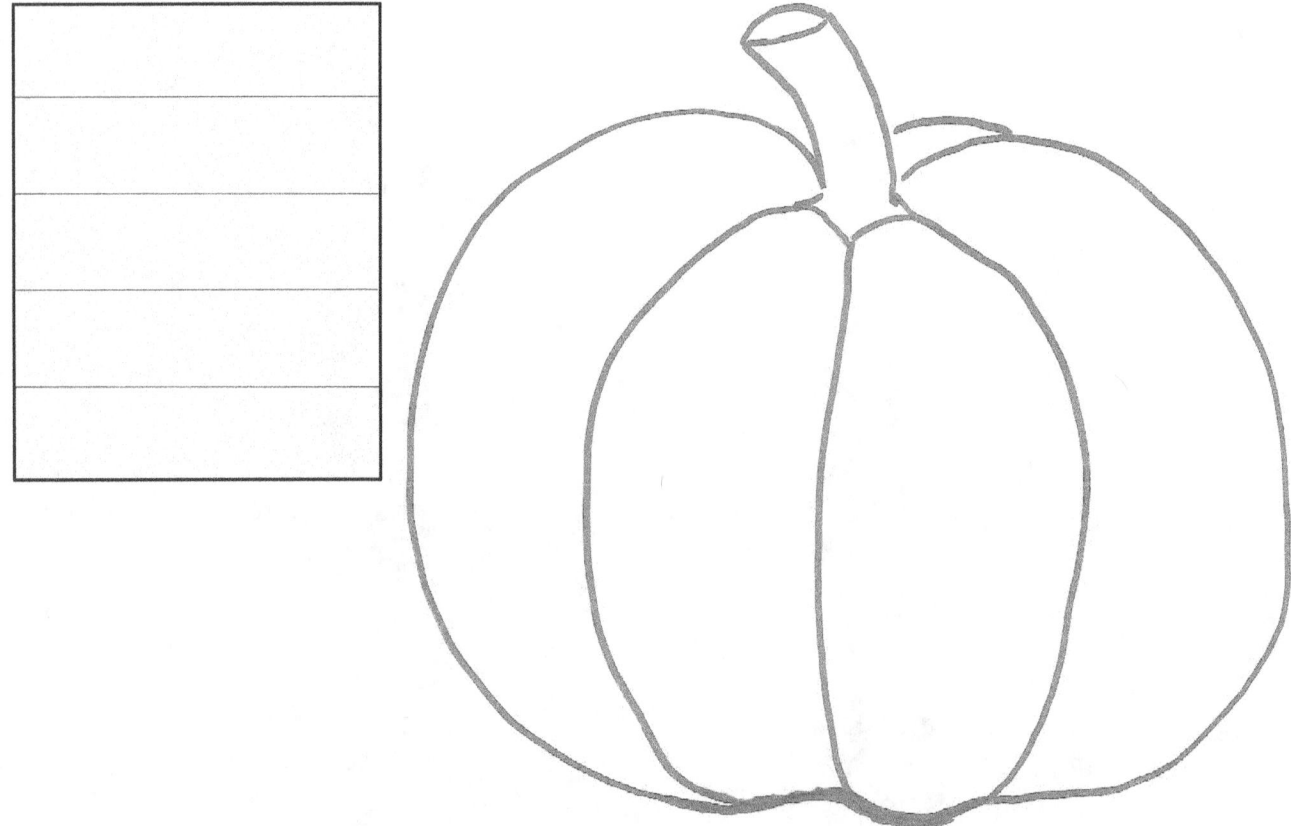

This is a pumpkin.
Dad picked the pumpkin.
Mom cooked the pumpkin.
Dad ate the pumpkin with butter.

Name: _____

Date: _____

These pictures have the letter-symbol **p** in their names. Find the letter-symbol **p** and color the **p** yellow.

pumpkin

octopus

parrot

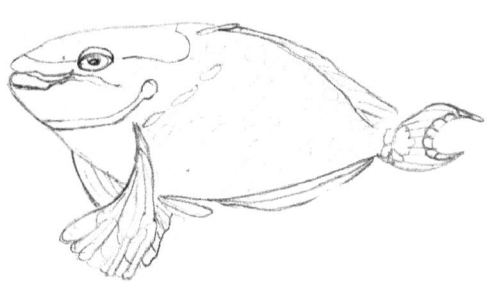

Spotlight Parrot fish

Name: _____

Date: _____

Color the picture frame.
Trace the letter-symbols.
Say the sound.
Write the letter-symbols.

uppercase R

lowercase r

Letter-symbol

r
R
rh
wr

You can hear the sound Rrrrrrr coming from the trooper's car.
Tell the story called "The R Troopers".

Name: _____

Date: _____

Draw a circle around the pictures and letter-symbols. Draw a line to match the pictures and letter-symbols. Say the sound for the letter-symbols as you draw the line.

r
R
rh

wr
R
r
rh

wr

Name: _____

Date: _____

Say the sound for the letter-symbols R, wr, rh, r. Circle the picture in each row that has that sound in its name.

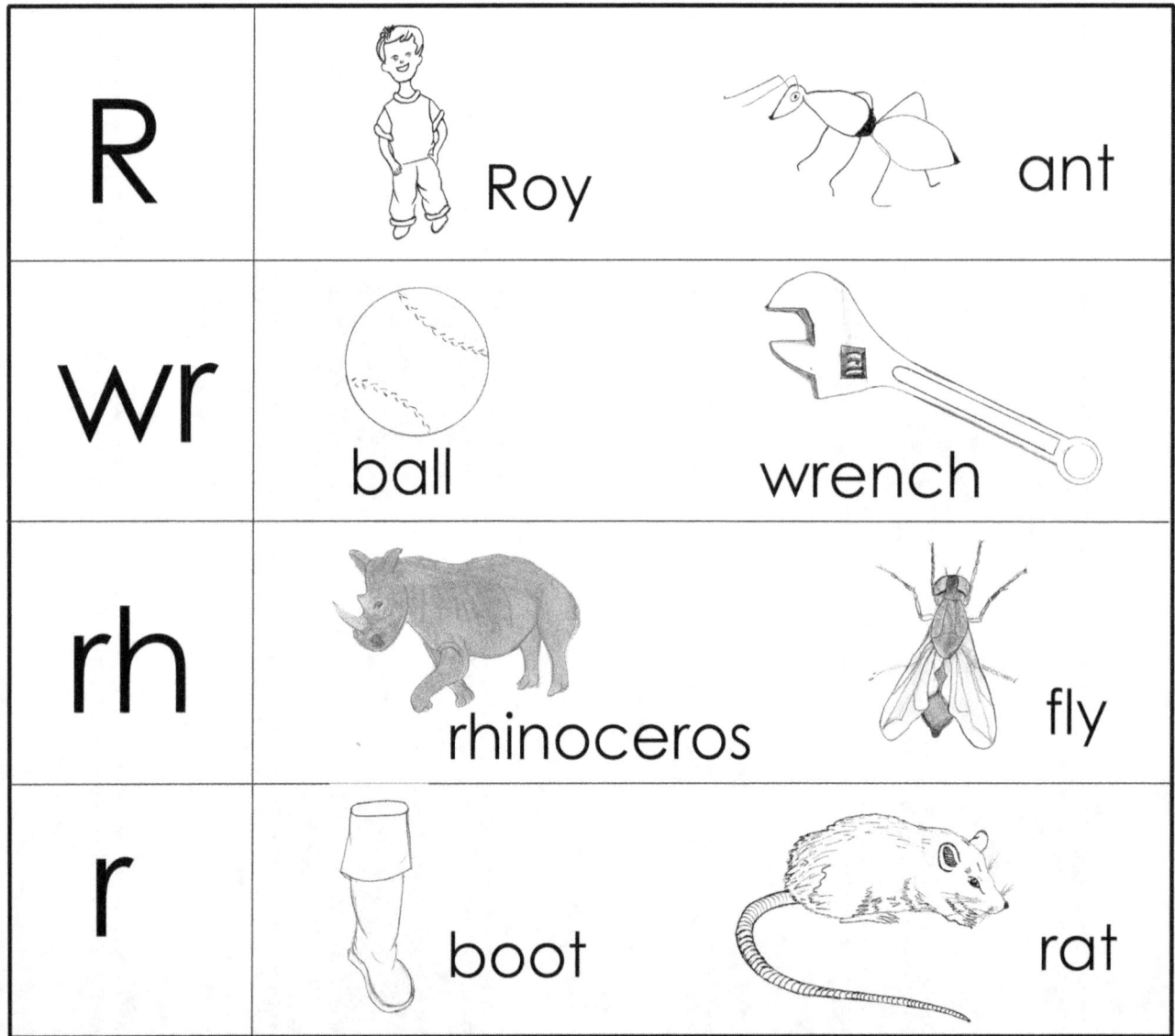

Name: _____

Date: _____

Color the picture of the **rh**inoceros.

This is a rhinoceros.
A rhinoceros eats plants.
It can swim and run fast.

Name: _____

Date: _____

Color the picture of the pa**rr**ot.

This is a parrot.
A parrot is a bird.
This parrot can sing.

Name: _____

Date: _____

Color the picture frame.
Trace the letter-symbols.
Say the sound.
Write the letter-symbols.

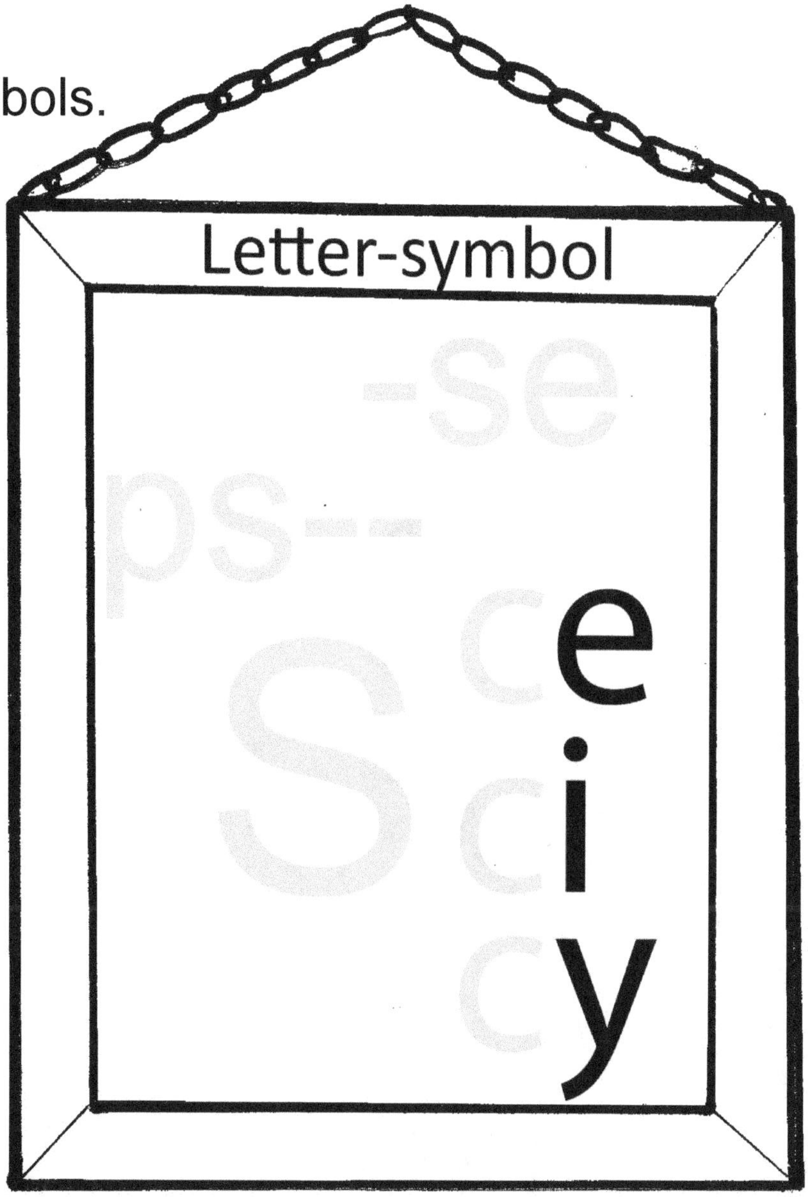

Letter-symbol

ps--se
S ce ce
e
i
c y

Name: _____

Date: _____

Draw a circle around the pictures and letter-symbols. Draw a line to match the pictures and letter-symbols. Say the sound for the letter-symbols as you draw the line.

s

-se   ps--

              s

ps--   -se

Name: _____

Date: _____

Draw a line to match the letter-symbol with the name of the picture.

ce

cylinder

ci

circle

cy

cellphone

When **e**, **i**, **y** come after the letter-symbol **c** the c makes a /s/ sound.

Name: _____

Date: _____

Say the sound for the letter-symbols S, se, ps. Circle the picture in each row that has that sound in its name.

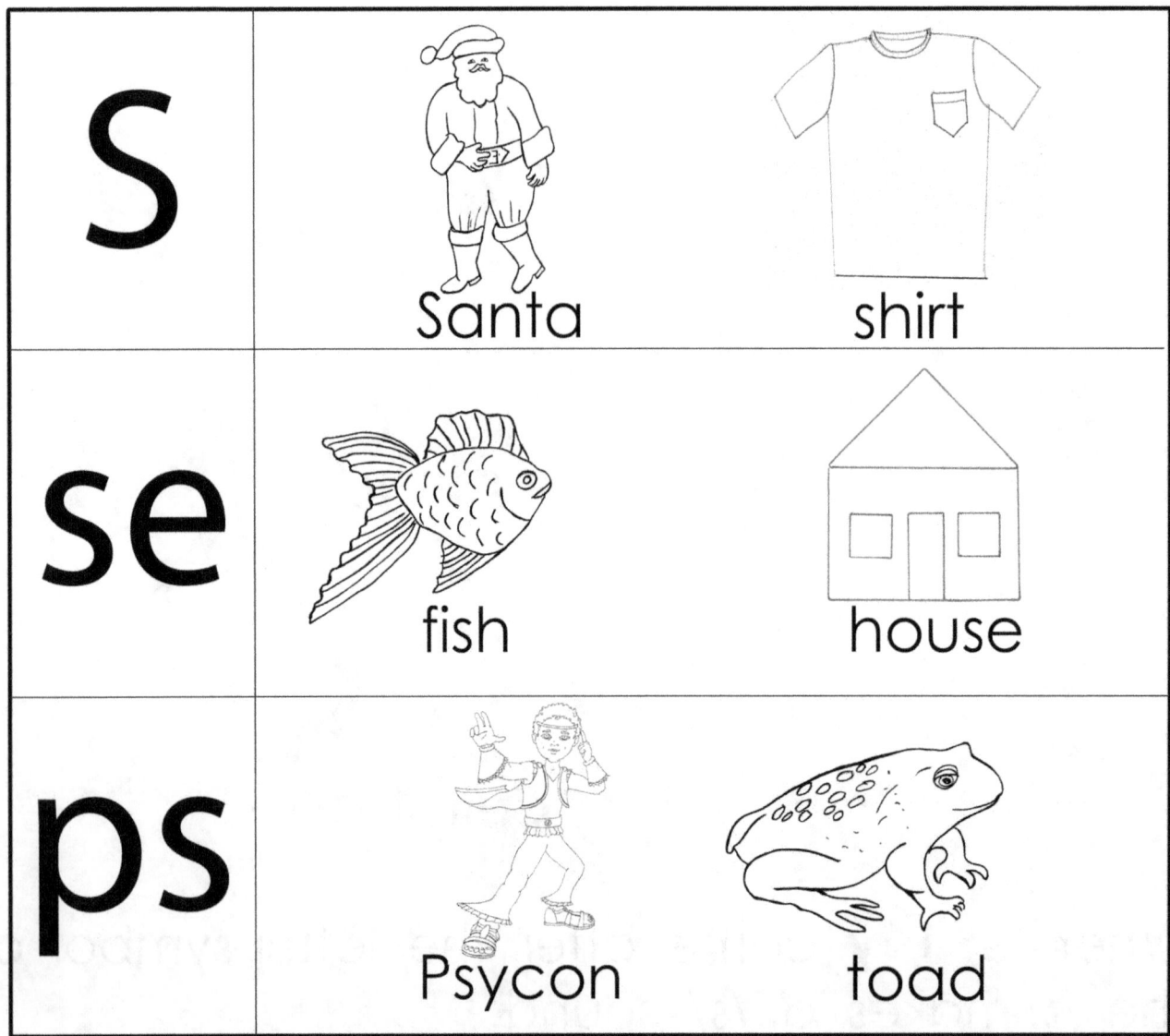

Name: _____

Date: _____

Color the picture of the **s**un.

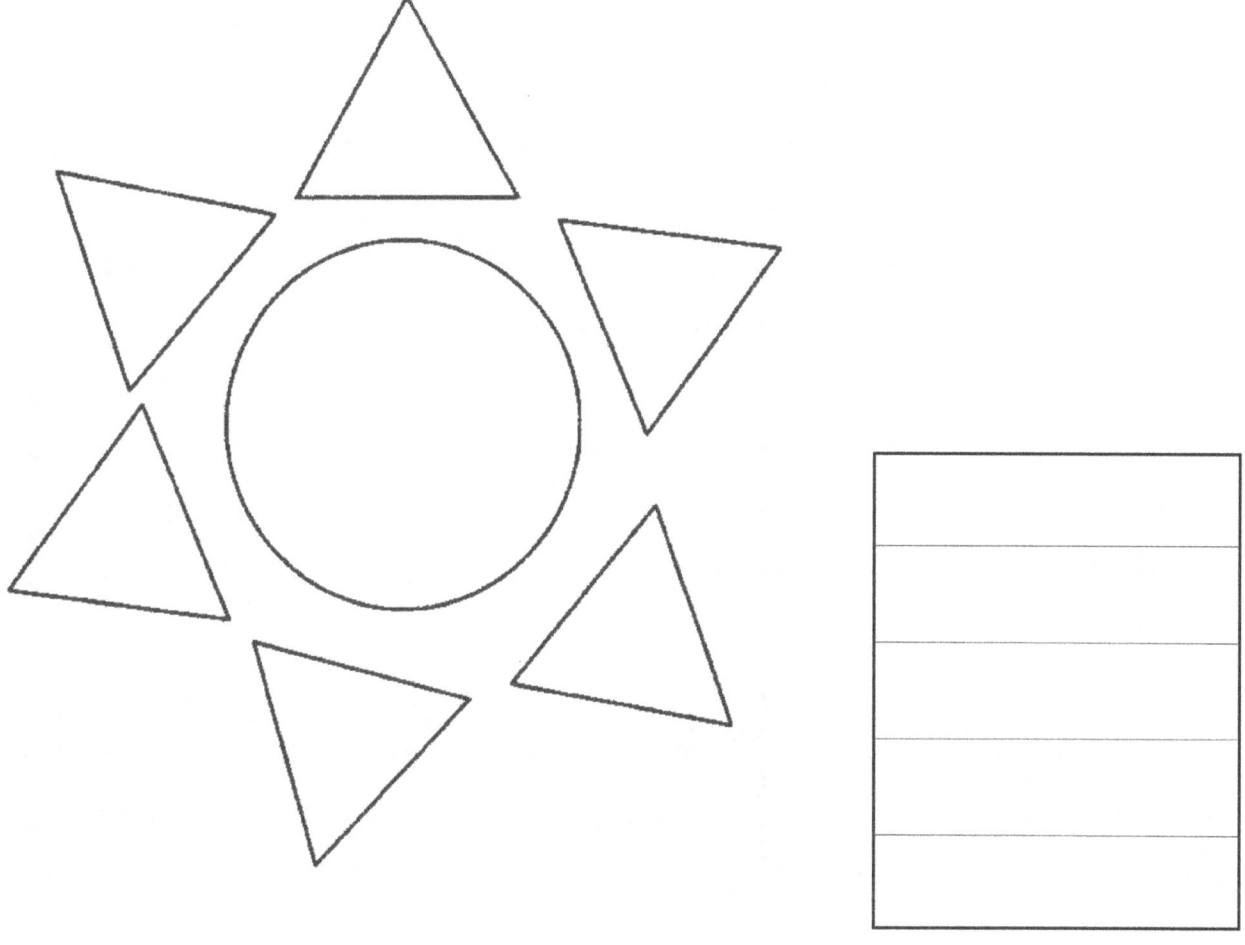

The sun is a big star.
We need the sunlight.
Plants need the sunlight.

Name: _____

Date: _____

Color the picture frame.
Trace the letter-symbols.
Say the sound.
Write the letter-symbols.

Letter-symbol

Sh

--- ti --

--- ci --

--- ssi --

"Sh! Be Very Quiet".
Now, tell the story about Psycon, the great one, in the Land of Make Believe.

Name: _____

Date: _____

Draw a circle around the pictures and letter-symbols. Draw a line to match the pictures and letter-symbols. Say the sound for the letter-symbols as you draw the line.

--ci--

Sh

---ti--

Sh

--ssi--

---ti--

--ssi--

--ci--

Name: _____

Date: _____

Say the /**sh**/ sound for the letter-symbols
sh, --ssi--, --ti--, --ci--.
Draw a line from the letter-symbol to the name of the picture that has the same letter-symbol.

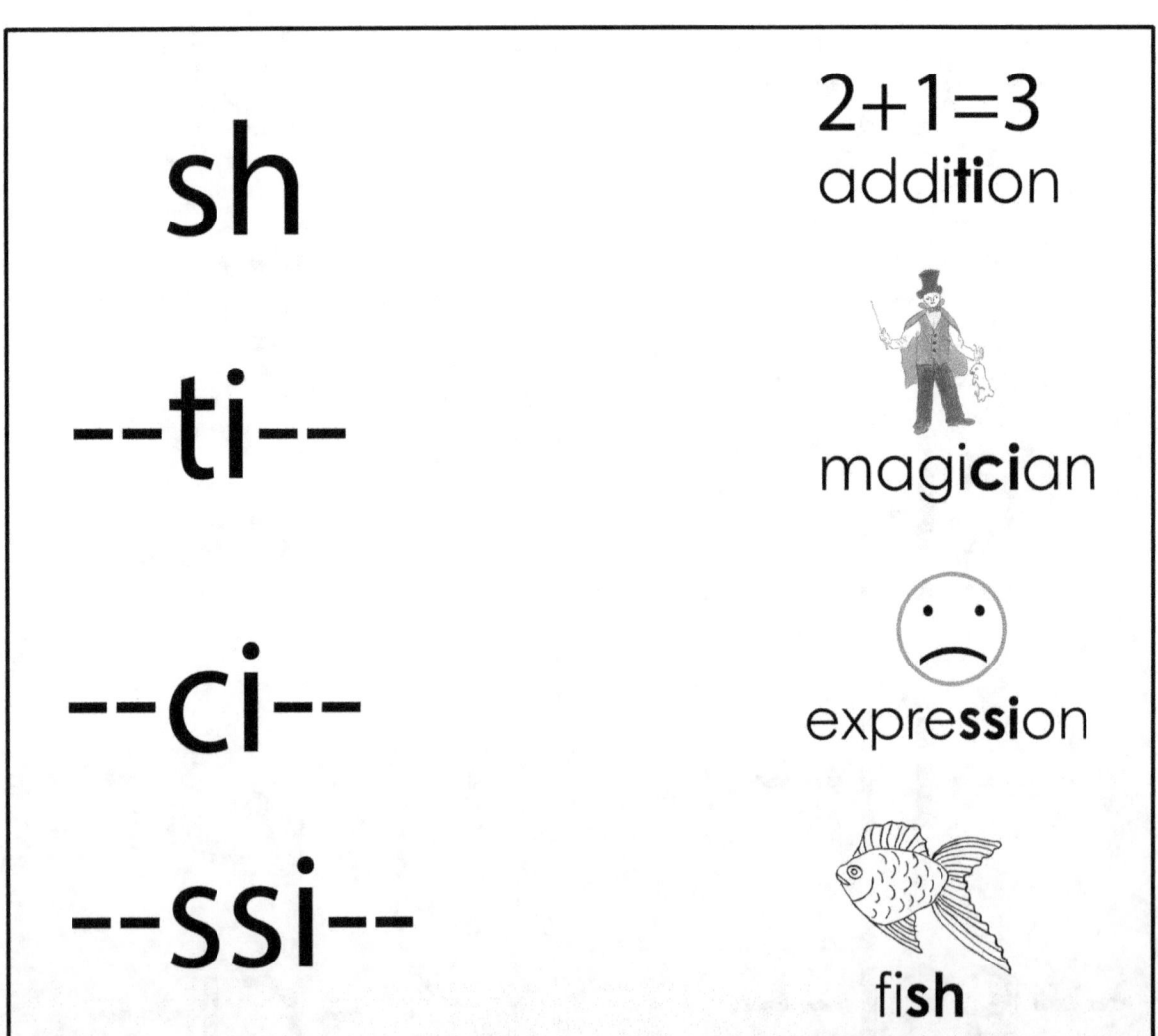

Name: _____

Date: _____

Find the words with the /sh/ sound in the puzzle and circle them.

```
s h i r t c i t
x i r t f i s h
a y s h o v e l
s h o e s h o p
```

 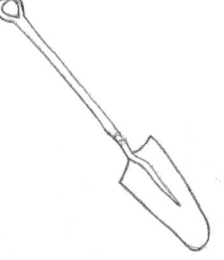 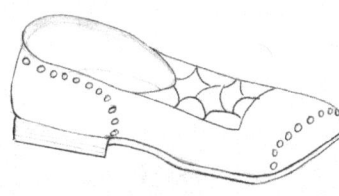

shirt   fish   shovel   shoe

Name: _____

Date: _____

Color the picture of the **sh**ell.

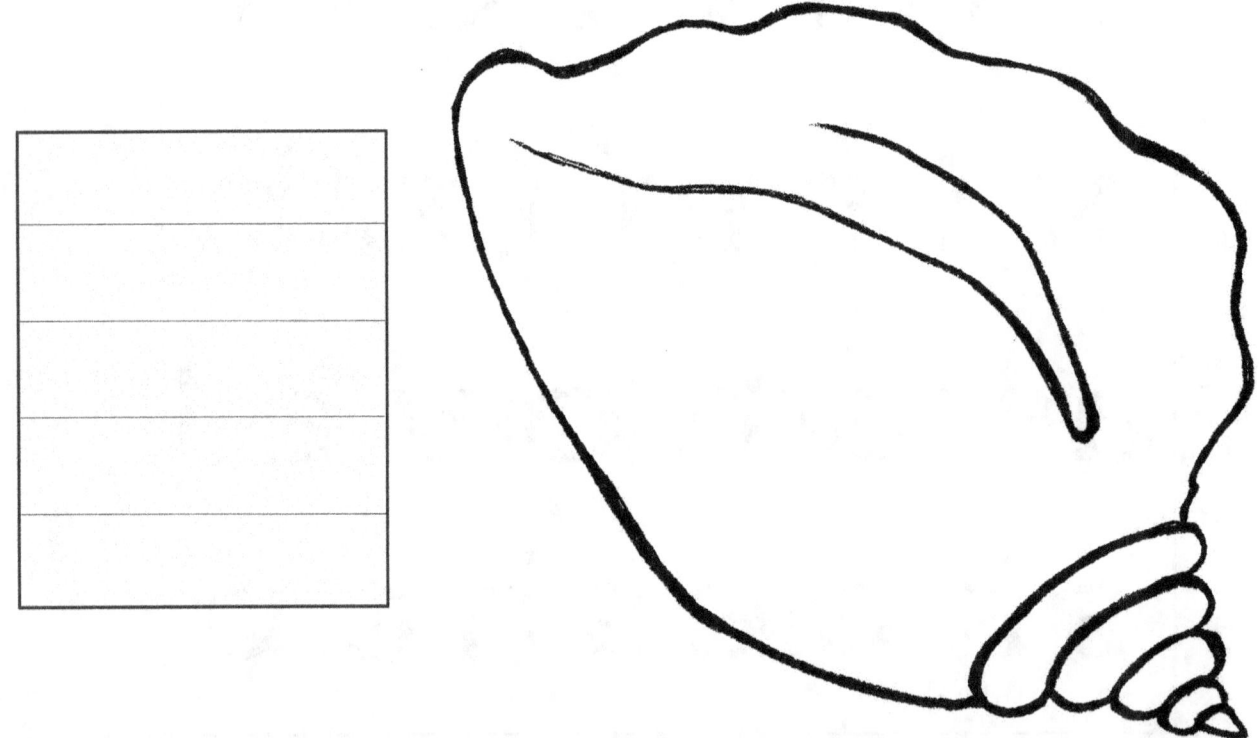

I saw a shell at the beach.
The shell has a pink color.
The shell is big.

Name: _____

Date: _____

Color the picture frame.
Trace the letter-symbols.
Say the sound.
Write the letter-symbols.

uppercase T
_____

lowercase t
_____

Letter-symbol

T t pt-

Tee Tee has a teapot, big and fat.
Tell the story "Tee Tee and the Teapot".

Name: _____

Date: _____

Draw a circle around the pictures and letter-symbols. Draw a line to match the pictures and letter-symbols. Say the sound for the letter-symbols as you draw the line.

Name: _____

Date: _____

Use a green crayon to draw uppercase **T** and lowercase **t** in the teapot.

Write these words on the line.

tea _____

pot _____

Tom _____

teapot _____

Teetee _____

Teetee has a teapot that is big and fat. Tom also has a teapot that is big and fat. Tom and Teetee's pots are full of green tea.

Name: _____

Date: _____

Color the picture frame.
Trace the letter-symbols.
Say the sound.
Write the letter-symbols.

uppercase Th
_____
_____

lowercase th
_____
_____

Letter-symbol

Th
th

Stick your tongue out and blow air. Try it!
Tell the story "T and h Two Good Friends".

Name: _____

Date: _____

Draw a circle around the pictures and letter-symbols. Draw a line to match the pictures and letter-symbols. Say the sound for the letter-symbols as you draw the line.

th

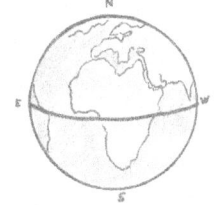

Th

th

Th

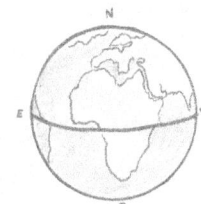

Name: _____

Date: _____

Find the letter-symbol **th** in these words and color them light green. Now read each word.

three   **th**em   mo**th**er

this   mou**th**   Ear**th**

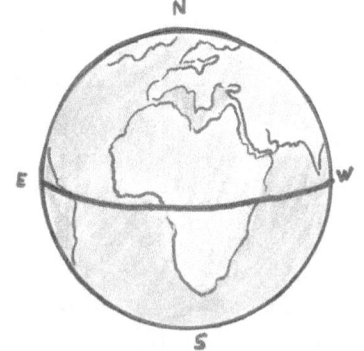

This is number three.
Count to three. 1 2 3
Color the number three.
Write the number three. _____

Name:

Date:

Color the picture frame.
Trace the letter-symbols.
Say the sound.
Write the letter-symbols.

Letter-symbol

uppercase U

lowercase u

"Phew P! Uh! Uh!" cries Mr. U-Vowel.
Tell the story "Mr. U-Vowel Goes Up".

Name: _____

Date: _____

Draw a circle around the pictures and letter-symbols. Draw a line to match the pictures and letter-symbols. Say the sound for the letter-symbols as you draw the line.

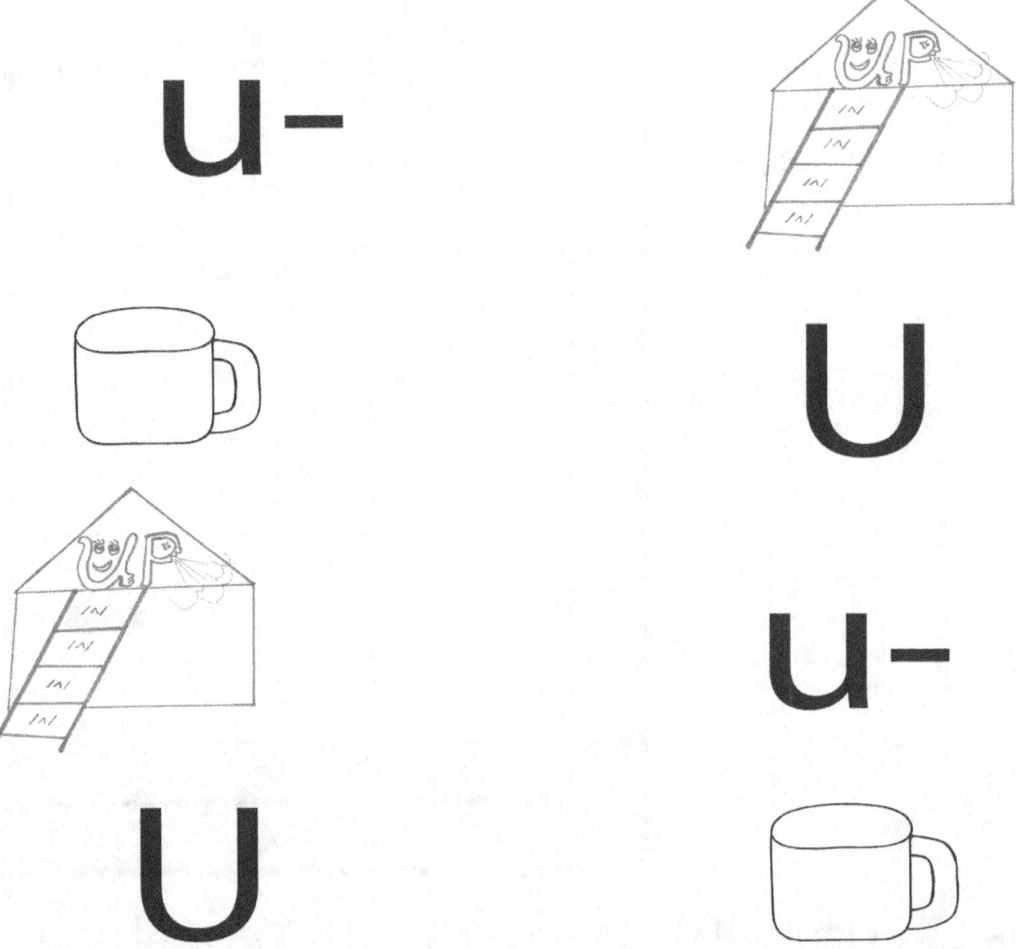

Name: _____

Date: _____

Color the picture.

Up, **U**p, **U**p Goes Mr. U-Vowel.
He goes to the top.
He meets Mr. P.

Name: _____

Date: _____

Write in the missing u-vowel symbol in the name of the picture.
Say the sound /**uh**/.
Color the pictures.

b___g

___mbrella

b___cket

d__ck

Name: _____

Date: _____

Color the picture frame.
Trace the letter-symbols.
Say the sound.
Write the letter-symbols.

Letter-symbol

ew
eu
ue
-u
u-e

_____
_____
_____
_____
_____
_____
_____
_____

Tell the story "Mr. U-Vowel".

Name: _____

Date: _____

Draw a circle around the pictures and letter-symbols. Draw a line to match the pictures and letter-symbols. Say the sound for the letter-symbols as you draw the line.

ew

eu

ew

eu

Find and color the letter-symbols **ew** and **eu** yellow.

Euro   newt   few   new

Name: _____

Date: _____

Draw a circle around the pictures and letter-symbols. Draw a line to match the pictures and letter-symbols. Say the sound for the letter-symbols as you draw the line.

ue   u-e

u-e   ue

Find and color the letter-symbols **ue u-e** yellow.

argue   use   mule   cue

Name: _____

Date: _____

Color the m**ule** brown.

This is a mule.
Dad has a mule.
Dad will use the mule for work.

Name:

Date:

Color the picture frame.
Trace the letter-symbols.
Say the sound.
Write the letter-symbols.

Letter-symbol

uppercase V

lowercase v

lowercase ve

V
-ve

Boy Van is the fastest creature.
Tell the story "Vvvvv Goes the Boy Van".

Name: _____

Date: _____

Draw a circle around the pictures and letter-symbols. Draw a line to match the pictures and letter-symbols. Say the sound for the letter-symbols as you draw the line.

-ve   V

V   -ve

Find and color the letter-symbols **V** and **-ve** in the words.

Van   vest   Bev   serve

Name: _____

Date: _____

Color the picture of the **v**est.

This is a vest.
Van has three vests.
Van has a black vest, a white vest and a brown vest.

Name: _____

Date: _____

Color the picture frame.
Trace the letter-symbols.
Say the sound.
Write the letter-symbols.

Letter-symbol

uppercase W
_____
_____

lowercase w
_____
_____

lowercase wh
_____
_____

W
w
wh

Wind provides energy for electricity.
Wind can dry our clothes.
Tell the story "W the Weatherman".

Name: _____

Date: _____

Draw a circle around the pictures and letter-symbols. Draw a line to match the pictures and letter-symbols. Say the sound for the letter-symbols as you draw the line.

wh   W

W   wh

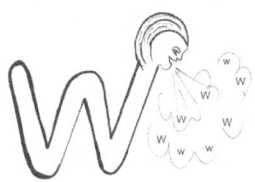   

Name: _____

Date: _____

Color the wagon red.
Color the wheels black.

This is my wagon.
I can put toys in it.
When I pull my wagon the wheels go round and round.

Name: _____

Date: _____

Color the picture frame.
Trace the letter-symbols.
Say the sound.
Write the letter-symbols.

Letter-symbol

uppercase Y
_____
_____

lowercase y
_____
_____

Y, the master of disguise, don't leave him out. He makes four sounds, /ee, igh, i, yee/.
Sing "The Vowel Song".

Name: _____

Date: _____

Draw a circle around the pictures and letter-symbols. Draw a line to match the pictures and letter-symbols. Say the sound for the letter-symbols as you draw the line.

y					Y

[picture]				y

Y					[picture]

The letter-symbol **Y** makes four sounds. Listen for the sounds **y** makes in these words. Color **y** yellow.

happy		my		gym		yes

Name: _____

Date: _____

Color the butterfly yellow.

This is a butterfly.
It is a big yellow butterfly.
It can fly very far.

Name: _____

Date: _____

Write the name for the picture:

... when **y** makes an "I" sound

fly
_____

... when **y** makes an "**ee**" sound"

happy
_____

... when **y** is a consonant

yarn
_____

Name: _____

Date: _____

Color the picture frame.
Trace the letter-symbols.
Say the sound.
Write the letter-symbols.

Letter-symbol

uppercase Z
_____
_____

lowercase z
_____
_____

lowercase x
_____
_____

Mr. Z takes his xylophone with him to the zoo.
Tell the story "Mr. Z-Consonant".

Name: _____

Date: _____

Draw a circle around the pictures and letter-symbols. Draw a line to match the pictures and letter-symbols. Say the sound for the letter-symbols as you draw the line.

Name: _____

Date: _____

Color the picture.

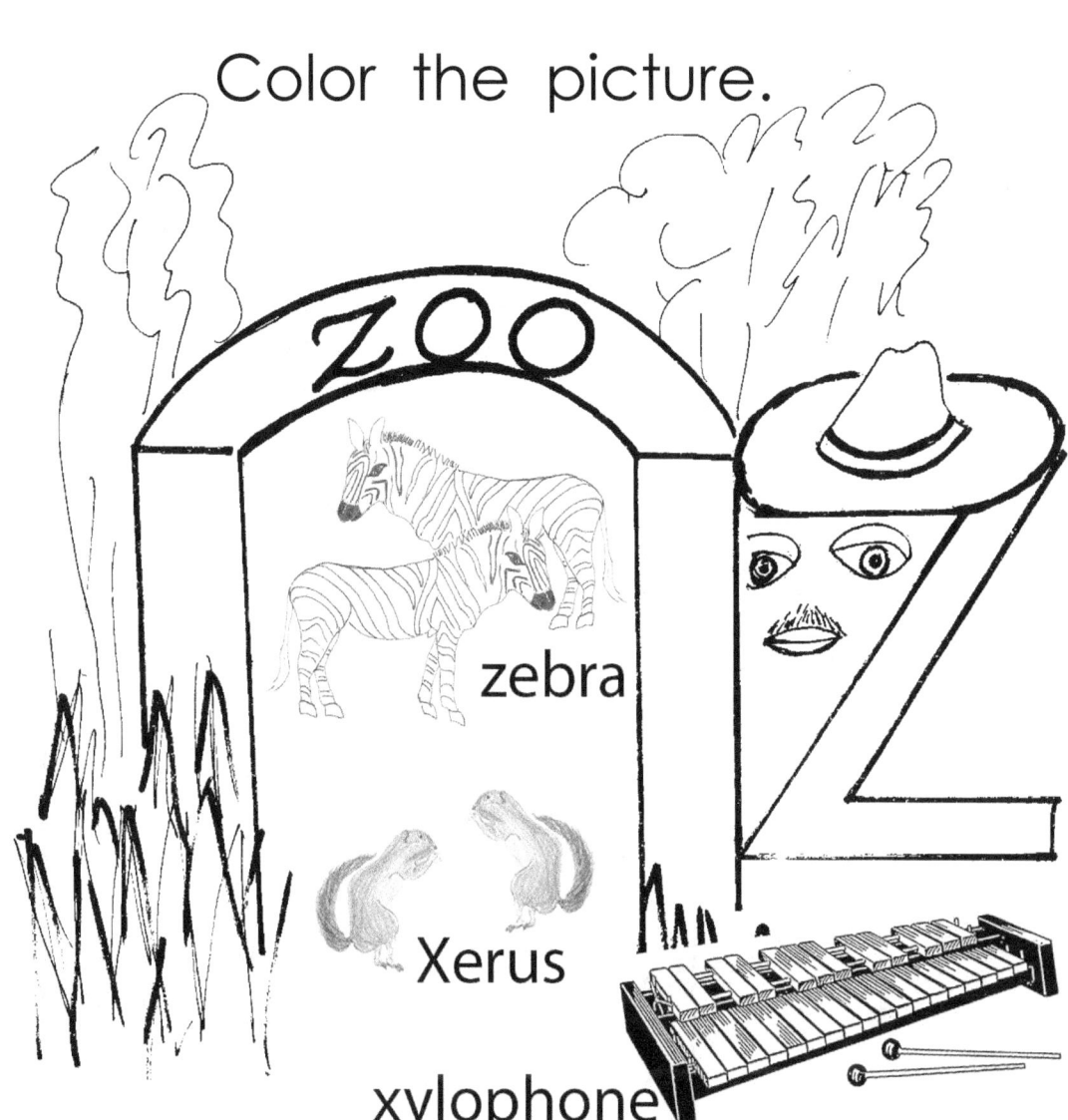

zebra

Xerus

xylophone

Color the **z** and **x** yellow in the name for the pictures. Say the names.
The **z** and **x** are making a /z/ sound.

Name:

Date:

Color the picture frame.
Trace the letter-symbols.
Say the sound.
Write the letter-symbols.

Letter-symbol

-si**a**
-si**on**
-s**ure**

When **-**s**ia -**s**ion -**s**ure** come at the end of a word the **si** and the **s** with **ure** after it make a **/zh/** sound.

Name: _____

Date: _____

Draw a circle around the pictures and letter-symbols. Draw a line to match the pictures and letter-symbols. Say the sound for the letter-symbols as you draw the line.

-sia

-sion   -sure

                -sia

-sure   -sion

Name: _____

Date: _____

Zh... Zh... Zh... Hop Aboard!

Color the imaginary machine.

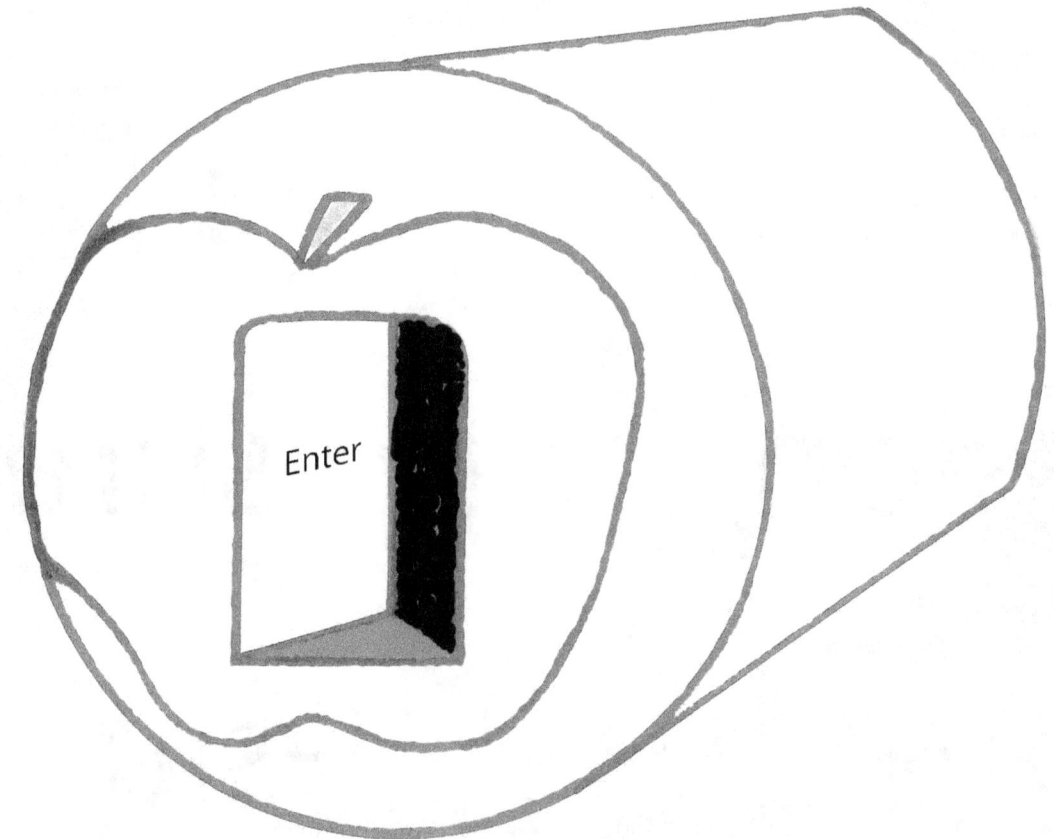

Color **-sia** **-sion** and **-sure** yellow in these words.

Asia   television   measure

Name: _____

Date: _____

Recognizing Words

Draw a line to match the words.

on	is
at	up
is	at
end	on
up	end

Name: _____

Date: _____

Patterns

What is next in the row?

Q U Q U Q ___

☐ ■ ☐ ■ ☐ ___

N E N E N ___

T I T I T ___

Name: _____

Date: _____

Patterns

What is next in the row?

B A B A B ___

● ○ ● ○ ● ___

p a p a p ___

O X O X O ___

Name: _____

Date: _____

Patterns

Use colors to make a pattern.

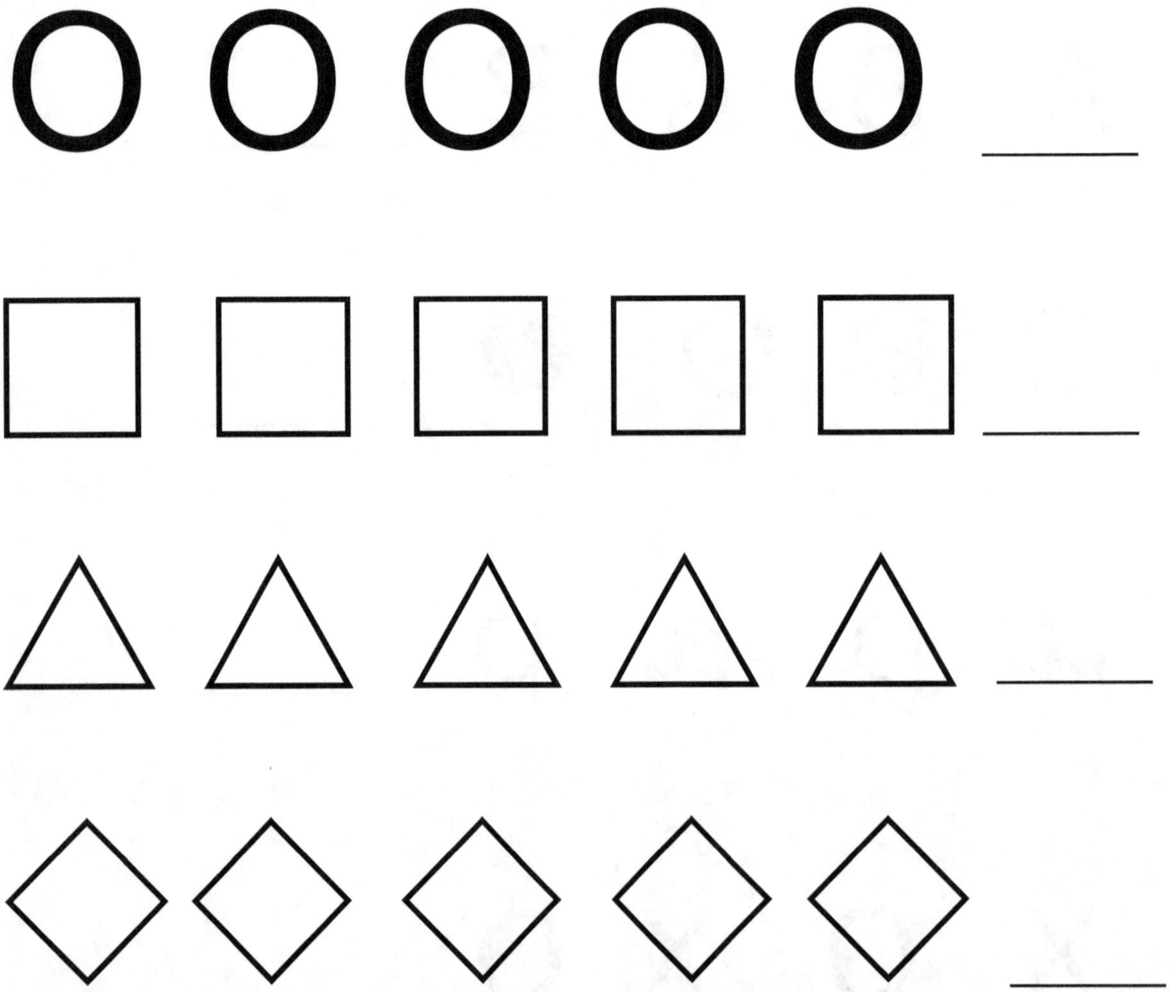

O O O O O O ___

☐ ☐ ☐ ☐ ☐ ___

△ △ △ △ △ ___

◇ ◇ ◇ ◇ ◇ ___

Name: _____

Date: _____

Introduction to the Land of Make Believe Jailhouse

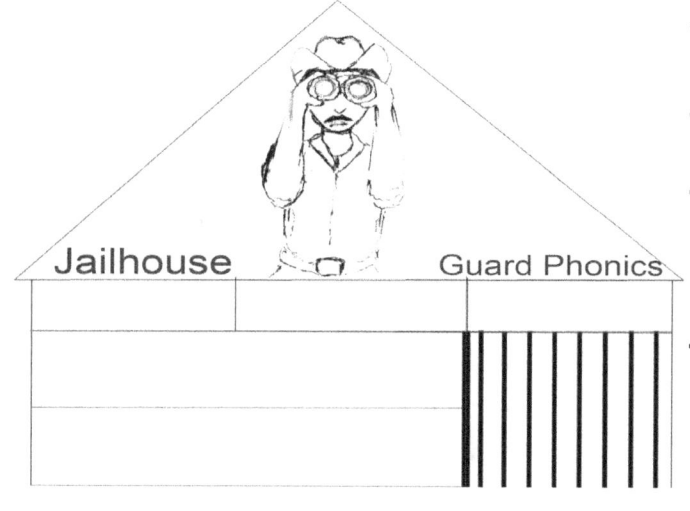

Words that break the rules are put in the jailhouse. We must remember these words and lookout for them.

Write our first two words in the Jailhouse.

w<u>a</u>s

| The letter-symbol **a** in w**a**s is making a short u-vowel sound as in up. |

<u>a</u>ll

| The letter-symbol **a** in **a**ll is making an aw sound as in awful. |

Name:

Date:

Put these words in the Jailhouse.

Jailhouse   Guard Phonics

me

the

we

he

she

be

equal

> Letter-symbol **e-vowel** is making a long **ee** vowel sound.

Date: _____

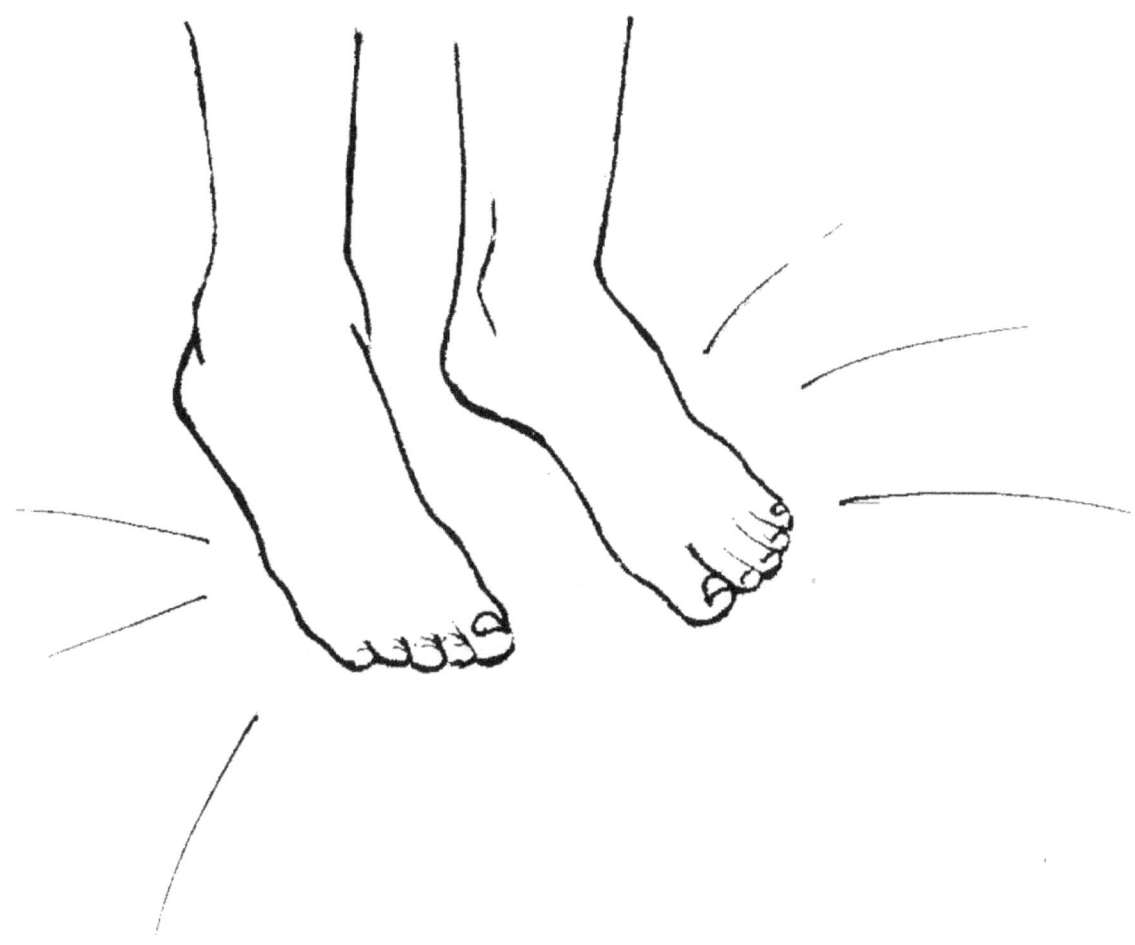

My Book Log

Title												Date Completed

Notes

www.ingramcontent.com/pod-product-compliance
Lightning Source LLC
Chambersburg PA
CBHW081352230426
43667CB00017B/2809